THE
HAPPINESS
HANDBOOK

THE
HAPPINESS
HANDBOOK

A Practical Guide to
Changing Your Life

DR. KEN HARMON
WITH **ASHLEY HARMON-POSTON**

Paperback ISBN: 979-8-9999238-0-6
Hardcover ISBN: 979-8-9999238-1-3

First Edition

This is a work of nonfiction. The authors have made every effort to ensure accuracy and completeness. However, the authors assume no responsibil-ity for errors, omissions, or outcomes resulting from the use of the infor-mation contained herein.

Book design by Alan Hebel
Printed in the United States of America

To my parents, Bill and Catherine Harmon, who gave me a wonderful life and consistently taught me to see the beauty in the world. And to my daughters, Ashley, Ava, and Norah, who remind me each day what a beautiful world it is.

— KEN

CONTENTS

The Birth of a Book 1
A Personal Note from Ashley 4
A Personal Note from Ken 7
How to Use This Book 11

SECTION 1

UNDERSTANDING YOUR HAPPINESS 13

Chapter 1: What You Think Makes You Happy 15
Chapter 2: Long Commutes, Money, and Memories 21
Chapter 3: Hedonic Adaptation 29
Chapter 4: The Arrival Fallacy 33
Chapter 5: The Happiness Percentage 39
Chapter 6: Those Happiness Rankings Don't Help 45

SECTION 2

WHAT TRULY MAKES YOU HAPPY 51

Chapter 7: Becoming a Great Drummer 53
Chapter 8: The Power of the Subconscious Mind 57
Chapter 9: The Subconscious and Happiness 63
Chapter 10: Do You Really Want to Be Happier? 67

SECTION 3
THE HAPPINESS LESSONS......73

Lesson 1: Start with Love......75
Lesson 2: Stop Complaining......81
Lesson 3: Stop Worrying......95
Lesson 4: Build Strong Relationships......105
Lesson 5: Say Thank You......113

A Final Word: What Makes You Happy? You!......123

THE BIRTH OF A BOOK

I was scheduled to give a happiness speech one evening in Bucharest, Romania. It was a dreary day with heavy rain, and in the afternoon my hosts came to me to apologize. I asked why they were apologizing, and they said because they were certain I would not have many people at my speech that evening. They said people would not venture out in such harsh weather for a speech. I told them it was absolutely no problem and we would have an enjoyable time even if only one person showed up. The evening came, I walked into the auditorium, and what did I see? A standing-room-only crowd! Yes, all the seats were full, and people were even standing around the back wall.

I want to be clear...this standing-room-only crowd had absolutely nothing to do with the fact I, Ken Harmon, was making a speech; I can guarantee they had no idea who I was. Instead, I realized they were there for one reason: Happiness!

This theme of people craving happiness has played out countless times over the years, showing people are hungry for Happiness. I often have civic organizations approach me about speaking at one of their meetings, and I will give them a choice of topics, including How to be a Great Leader, Human Relations, How to Develop a Strong Corporate Culture, or Happiness. They inevitably choose Happiness.

On a Friday afternoon in a cabin in Blue Ridge, Georgia, Ashley and I sat down to see if we could make progress on a book I had been writing for years. The title of the book was *Managing Happiness*, and its theme was to blend the research on happiness with leadership lessons. I had been writing the *Managing Happiness* book for years and needed to complete it, so I reached out to Ashley for help. She is brilliant (I know I'm a biased father, but it is objectively true), she is an excellent writer, and she understands me, three things I needed to complete this book. And even though Ashley, like me, is a CPA, she has a remarkably diverse background, a large view of life, and a passion for, and history of, coaching and helping people get more out of life. (I must interject a brag about Ashley here. Yes, she is a CPA, but she is also a certified life coach, a certified nutritionist, a certified yoga instructor, and a former NFL cheerleader.)

On the first day in the cabin, Ashley sat down with her computer and asked me to just start talking, so I started pacing back and forth, as I am inclined to do, and started talking. One of the first things I told her was the story about the speech in Romania and the fact everybody seems to want to focus exclusively on happiness. Her immediate, pivotal response was, "Then why don't we just write a handbook that teaches people how to be happier? We could call it The Happiness Handbook." I use the word "pivotal" because that moment changed everything. It gave us a zealous focus on happiness. I love helping companies develop great culture and helping leaders improve, but undoubtedly my greatest love is teaching people how to be happier. At that moment, this book was born.

Based on the feedback I have received in my speeches over the years, everyone has clear ideas about what would make them happy, and they take actions every day based on those ideas. However, most people also say they are not happy or would like to be happier. They know what makes them happy, yet happiness is elusive. Could it be their ideas about what would make them happy are wrong?

The truth is most people simply do not understand happiness, and the things they think make them happy do not. Most people never received guidance on how to achieve happiness. They instead relied on various societal influences to tell them what brings happiness. They learned happiness from parents, friends, the news, and advertising. The happiness research, though, reveals those lessons learned from societal influences are wrong and do not lead to greater happiness. Most people haven't had the chance to learn what they can do each day to be happier.

That is why Ashley and I wrote this handbook. We think it's time for everyone to learn how to be happy. The lessons in this book are based on extensive findings from brilliant researchers. We break down that research to give you simple, practical guidance you can use every day. One thing we can promise you is that if you practice the steps we describe, you will be happier. In fact, you will be measurably happier in a short period of time, and your happiness will continue to grow.

We promise these lessons work!

We promise the process is fun!

Happy reading!

Ken and Ashley

A PERSONAL NOTE FROM ASHLEY

Right around the time Dad and I got serious about this book, I ended up at a workshop focused on leading with vulnerability. The location wasn't glamorous, and you can probably picture it...a huge, bland conference room with eight of us sitting at round tables we had to make our way to after a break. I truly was very excited about this topic (I've always been Ken Harmon's daughter after all). However, as someone who can't sit still and has to talk to as many people as possible in between sessions, I ended up at one of those "coveted" round table seats with my back facing the speakers.

Picture me, the Type A, eldest daughter I am, with my notebook and pen ready to go, eyes (unfortunately) locked in on the back wall. Still, the speakers sucked me in immediately, and as I was furiously scribbling pages of notes with my back turned toward them, they asked how many of us were raised to think vulnerability is a good thing. Without a second thought, I shot my hand up, not even pausing to put my pen down. The silence in the room was deafening as I realized everyone was looking in my direction. In a room of nearly 200 people, I was the only one raising my hand.

I can say with 99.99% certainty this was <u>not</u> what the speakers had prepared for. My guess is this was supposed to be a scripted moment when no one in the room raised their hand. They ended up rolling with the curveball I accidentally threw them beautifully, asking me with genuine shock:

"WHO ARE YOUR PARENTS?" They rolled with it so well and led such a great discussion afterwards that I was able to ignore the fact I had essentially hijacked their presentation for what felt like the longest two minutes of my life. Since I could ignore it, I figured others would as well. But then (over wine) later, I had countless people pull me aside and tell me: "I didn't even have to turn around. I knew it was you."

As I reflected back on the moment and the wine-fueled chats after, something clicked for me. In a room of so many successful, inspiring professionals, I was the ONLY one who grew up in a vulnerable household. Not only that, somehow in that room, I was the only one who so many others thought of when the topic was raised. That day gave me the opportunity to both see for myself and share with others how grateful I am to have grown up in a home where vulnerability was the norm. My parents always taught me to feel my feelings and uncomfortable feelings were never bad or shameful. They're just...feelings.

Okay, now let me acknowledge what you might be thinking right now: "Ashley, this book is about HAPPINESS, not vulnerability." To that I would say: allowing yourself to be happy means being vulnerable. It doesn't mean everything is perfect, but it means making a choice every day to sit with the uncomfortable feelings, to acknowledge the sometimes really sh*tty circumstances, and decide to control the narrative. That decision makes you a better friend, employee, leader, partner, parent...I could go on and on. And it's one only YOU can make.

With that, in the spirit of vulnerability, it feels like a perfect time to interrupt this story and share a little Harmon family secret: Dad hasn't always been "The Happiness Guy." Don't get me wrong; to me, he's the ultimate girl dad, and he's always been happiness, love, and passion in human form. But Dad didn't always practice what he preaches. It took a series of transformative life events, ones that are his stories to tell, for him to start living his own lessons and listening to the advice he's been sharing with me and my sisters for as long as I can remember. Those events, the ones I sometimes wasn't sure if he would recover from, also let my Dad become "The Happiness Guy" who is writing this book.

Teenage Ashley would hate me for saying this, but I can finally admit he's always known the answers. She also would love for me to tell you this was my plan all along. But I can't lie to you. The moment in the mountains we told you about didn't happen because I suggested it...it only happened because Dad was ready. Because he had finally lived it. Now, after years of him making sure his girls never had to doubt how proud he is of us, I get to tell the world how proud I am of him. I'm not just proud of him for this book (which is pretty exciting, don't get me wrong). It's because he's himself. He's HAPPY, and because he's taught me well, there's nothing more I could want for him.

I truly couldn't be more excited for you to experience the same happiness I've known my entire life. I think my sisters would agree that being in the inner circle with us "Harmon Girls" is a pretty great place to be.

Ashley

A PERSONAL NOTE FROM KEN

I have a confession: I am an accountant. I have three degrees in accounting, have worked as a CPA, and have been an accounting professor for years. Why would an accountant write a happiness book, and perhaps more important, why would you want to read a happiness book written by an accounting professor?

Twenty years ago, I attended a leadership course delivered by one of the most prominent leadership training firms in the world. It was a full-week, residency-based program with about 40 participants from different industries. Before we arrived for the week, we each took a series of personality and leadership assessments that the training firm's staff psychologists reviewed. Those psychologists would not only review our assessments; they would also see how the assessments aligned with our performance during the week.

On the last day of the program, each of us sat down for an extended one-on-one session with one of the psychologists. On the day of my meeting, I walked in the door and strolled across a large room toward the psychologist, who was sitting in a chair and flipping through an exceptionally large loose-leaf binder. The binder contained detailed analysis of me, my assessments, and my performance during the week. As I approached the psychologist, she held up her hand and said, "Before you even sit down, I have one primary question. Why in the hell are you an accountant?" I shrugged and laughed, and she laughed, too. She went on to say my personality profile was the exact opposite of what they typically see in accountants and therefore assumed I would not be happy as an accountant. As she continued, I could not argue the point. I then explained I saw myself more as a professor than an accountant.

As a professor, I like to make concepts, even exceedingly difficult concepts, "Harmon simple." This means I like to break concepts into digestible, understandable bites and then help others build their knowledge with those bites so they can ultimately grasp the difficult concept. This process applies to various areas of my life, including my teaching, my leadership coaching, and now my happiness instruction.

You might logically ask why I got into the world of happiness. I will take you back to 2009, when a university in Romania asked me to teach a leadership course in their Executive MBA program. I was a business dean at the time and had been in various leadership positions over the years and had attended various leadership development programs. As I prepared to teach, my initial thought was to get an excellent textbook on leadership. I gathered title suggestions from colleagues and conducted my own research. I then started ordering various leadership books. Some of the books were excellent, but none of them struck a chord with me, so I kept discarding them. They seemed to focus on steps leaders should take or taxonomies of what leaders do. Deep in my heart, though, I always thought great leadership was mostly about who you are as a person. I didn't think these books addressed what I saw as a crucial element of leadership.

Around that same time, I happened to hear an interview with the brilliant happiness researcher and author, Dan

Gilbert. Dr. Gilbert had published his seminal work, *Stumbling on Happiness*,[1] a few years before, and in the interview, he summarized the book's key elements, such as what truly makes people happy and what does not make them happy. His book is based on his years of research in the happiness and positive-psychology arenas and to say its findings are shocking and life changing would be an understatement.

That evening, I was reflecting on Dr. Gilbert's book, and I then realized I may have found an essential element for teaching leadership. The happiness literature shows us that we can transform who we are and transform how we engage with the world, and to me these are crucial elements for great leadership. From that moment, I decided to use more of a psychological approach to leadership and incorporate lessons on happiness.

I can honestly say my life changed at that moment. I became infatuated with happiness research and started looking for ways I could break down that research into digestible pieces and make them "Harmon Simple." I've had the immense joy of helping people use happiness to change their lives for more than 15 years. I have had the great fortune to deliver hundreds of happiness talks in seven countries, and based on the feedback I've received even years later, I know those talks changed some lives...including mine.

I took the happiness lessons and put them into my speeches, coaching, and consulting. Most importantly, though, I put those happiness lessons into practice in my own life. This is where the personal note becomes a little more personal. My life has had some challenges in recent years. My best friend of 50 years, David Davis, died in a motorcycle crash (yes, I still ride motorcycles...one of David's enduring lessons was to keep on living and riding), I went through a divorce, I had two types of cancer (I am fully recovered now), I stepped down from a leadership role after 24 years in various leadership roles, and more recently, my mother passed away. I tell you these stories not to garner your sympathy. Far from it, these events are part of life. I instead reveal these challenges because they helped me appreciate the power of the lessons in this book. As you may imagine, each of these "life circumstances" brought sadness, great sadness at times, but the lessons in this book helped me navigate those moments and bring me to an even better place afterward. When people ask how I am doing, I can honestly say I have never been more at peace in my life. I am genuinely happy.

Because I have lived the lessons in this book, I am even more excited to reveal the lessons to you. I obviously cannot promise you a life without challenges or sadness. After all, the beauty of life is that we face challenges, manage those challenges, learn from those challenges, and come out better on the other side. As you implement the happiness lessons, you will have greater progress some days than others and might even have setbacks, but I promise you these lessons will give you a path to greater happiness. These lessons changed my life. I only want that for you.

Ken

HOW TO USE THIS BOOK

Since that fateful day when Ashley suggested we write *The Happiness Handbook*, we have been driven by one goal: to give simple, executable, daily lessons that will make you happier. These lessons are in Section 3 of this book, but to give context to the lessons, Sections 1 and 2 contain information to help you develop a deeper understanding of what does not make you happy, what does make you happy, and how your brain works. You can then use this knowledge to understand why we are giving you the lessons in Section 3 and why they work.

You might enjoy trying numerous lessons at a time, but we suggest you focus on one lesson at a time. The "homework assignments" at the end of each lesson ask you to describe how you are going to implement each lesson. There's also an assignment asking you to reflect on your experience with the lesson and note any progress you have had and any challenges you faced. The assignments help you guide yourself on what works best for you. You will find a single lesson takes weeks or even months to implement fully. That's okay. The most important "assignment" is to be patient with yourself and enjoy the ride. The purpose of the book is to change your life, and simply starting the journey is a beautiful beginning to that change.

SECTION 1

UNDERSTANDING YOUR HAPPINESS

"Most people wake up every day and work against their own happiness."

CHAPTER 1

WHAT YOU THINK
MAKES YOU HAPPY

Take a few minutes to think about your happiness and write down three things that make you happy. I have assigned this same task at my speeches for the last 15 years. As you do this exercise yourself, I think you will find it brings smiles and fond reflections as you think about all the things in life that make you happy. When I do this in person, I ask for volunteers to share just one of the items on their list. With a big smile, someone will shout out, "My grandchildren!" And then another will say, "Reading a book" or "My dog." Over those 15 years of giving happiness speeches, I have given this assignment in multiple countries with a wide array of cultures. Regardless of culture or country, though, the answers remain surprisingly similar. Here is a sample of what I have heard:

- A day at the beach
- My children
- My grandchildren
- Listening to music
- Playing music
- My dog

- My friends
- A quiet evening
- Reading a book
- Time in nature
- Dancing

I recently had an unusual, yet wonderful, response that I had not encountered before. In a speech to a university leadership team, one gentleman in the audience excitedly responded, "Competition!" I assumed he was an athlete who had a competitive spirit, so I asked him what sport he played. He said, "Oh, I'm not an athlete; I just like to be in competition with myself to be the best I can be." I loved this response!

Now that you have had fun thinking of three things that make you happy, I have a more advanced assignment. Please take a few minutes to contemplate and then write down three things that would make you happier. When I give this advanced assignment in my speeches, the audience immediately gets quiet, and their faces look more serious. It's fun to think about happiness, but people truly struggle to produce a definitive answer about what would make them happier.

I typically give them a little more time and then ask if someone is willing to share just one thing that would make them happier. Some responses are lighthearted, such as:

- I would be happier if I had a car that worked.
- I would be happier if I lived at the beach.
- I would be happier if I traveled more.

But the answers can sometimes be a little more serious:

- I would be happier if my son could find a job.
- I would be happier if I could buy a house.
- I would be happier if I could get out of debt.

Sometimes the responses have been notably serious and moving:

- I would be happier if my husband were in remission from his cancer.

- I would be happier if I could walk on my own again.

I have noticed there is one answer to this question that occurs more than any other, regardless of country or culture, and that answer is: "More time." Wanting more time has considerable depth and often means different things to different people, but for most "more time" means having enough time for both family and work. They seem frustrated with the competing demands of life, and they see the struggle to fulfill all obligations of work, family, and leisure as making them unhappy. They logically conclude "more time" would allow the struggles to lessen and accordingly make them less stressed and happier.

I will occasionally have someone in the audience hesitantly say, "I would be happier if I had more money." When someone has the courage to admit this, the other audience members will inevitably applaud and feel relieved. This tells me those other audience members were thinking the same thing but were hesitant to say it. They have all heard the phrase, "Money can't buy happiness," which is mostly true, but deep down they do not believe it. I imagine you, too, have had fun imagining what you would do if you won a huge lottery prize. You think about cars, jets, homes, and travel. I also imagine you picture yourself without any care in the world and beaming with happiness.

If you did think "more money" would make you happier, you might not imagine needing millions. Instead, you might view "more money" like "more time." Just a little more money, like a little more time, would help you conquer your daily struggles. More money would help you meet monthly expenses, save for college, pay for vacations, and prepare for retirement. These financial demands can bring worry and stress, so it's logical to conclude additional money would solve or lessen these problems and therefore bring greater happiness. The research conclusively shows more money (even winning millions in the lottery) does not bring more happiness, but it's easy to see the logic that reduced stress about money would bring additional happiness.

I assume it was fun to think about things that make you happy and things that would make you happier. If you are like others I have encountered over the years, your answers brought you feelings of joy. It is appropriate to feel joy while reflecting on days at the beach, time with grandchildren, or sitting quietly with a glass of wine and a book. They are wonderful and can bring moments of joy, but do they lead to lasting happiness? Unfortunately, the answer is no.

To drive this point further, consider an unusual question. It is an adaptation of a question asked by the great happiness researcher, Dr. Daniel Gilbert.[2] The question is: Which of the following events would make you happier? (a) Breaking your leg or (b) Spending a week on the Greek Island of Santorini. Your response might be, "That's a stupid question," and I agree it appears to be. If you had the choice of breaking your leg or spending time on Santorini, I hope you would choose Santorini. But the question is not which of these events you would choose; instead, the question is which of these events would make you happier. The answer will be revealed later in the book (this is where we tease you to keep you reading).

The quote at the beginning of this section says: "Most people wake up every day and work against their own happiness." The quote is my own and is the result of watching human behavior the many years I have been promoting happiness. From what I have seen, people get up in the morning, go through their daily routines, and assume their stresses and struggles are leading to a place of greater happiness. I always wonder if they would change their focus if they knew the path was not leading to greater happiness.

Happiness can be hard to achieve if you have never learned how to be happy. You developed your assumptions about happiness from messages delivered by advertising, social media, family, and peers. These messages became part of your subconscious, and you are heading down a path you think leads to happiness. The path leads somewhere, but the odds are it doesn't lead to happiness. This book is your first step to learning how to be happy. The lessons in this book can lead you down a different path, a beautiful path toward lasting happiness.

CHAPTER 2

LONG COMMUTES, MONEY, AND MEMORIES

I was provost of a large university in Metro Atlanta. Let me just stop here and admit this was one of the most difficult jobs I ever had. The job itself was not difficult; it was delightful. The difficulty came from telling people what I did for a living. I could be attending a reception, and someone would ask what I do for a living. I would enthusiastically answer, "I'm a provost." Their typical response was a blank stare, and then the brave question, "What's a provost?" To quote the legendary humorist, Dave Barry, "Let's say you're a university provost. You can deduct any expense you want (on your taxes), because nobody has a clue what 'provost' means." [3] I won't bore you with the academic definition of a provost; let's just say a provost typically is the vice president in charge of all things academic at a university. Now you know.

Now, back to the story. The university where I was provost sat in the suburbs of Atlanta, and my office was right next to Interstate 75, which leads into the city. If you know anything about Atlanta and its notorious traffic issues, you can guess what I saw every morning on the interstate. If you guessed that I "saw lots of happy people," you would be wrong. However, they did seem to have a tradition of "waving" at each other.

Each morning, I would see long lines of cars creeping down the interstate at a snail's pace or even sitting at a dead standstill. What do you think their response would have been if I had walked out there on the interstate, tapped on someone's window, and asked, "What are you doing today to pursue happiness?" They might give me one of those "waves," but I imagine the most common response would be, "Why do you think I'm sitting here in this traffic? This is how I am pursuing happiness!" They might then explain they are pursuing happiness by battling traffic each day so they can have a job that pays enough to support them and their family. As they see it, they need the money to take family vacations, buy a larger home, send their kids to college, or buy a new car that is reliable. If I asked why they simply do not move closer to their work, they might say they can get a bigger house farther out in the suburbs or they like the schools in those suburbs. They assume that by providing for themselves and their family, they will attain happiness. Providing for family and having goals of houses, trips, vacations, and cars are admirable, but unfortunately those things do not lead to lasting happiness.

After relocating to Atlanta, I spoke with friends and neighbors about their commutes, and they shocked me with their responses. They would describe commutes of one or two hours each way, every day. I know long commutes are not unusual in large cities, but I still find it amazing people sit in their cars for three hours or more each day just to go back and forth to work. When I probe my Atlanta friends some more, they tell me living closer to their work is prohibitively expensive, they like the schools in the suburbs, and they can have a nicer house out in the suburbs. Their underlying assumption is that they achieve an equilibrium, or an equal tradeoff, between the stresses of fighting a long commute each day and the benefit of more money, better schools, and a nice house. The happiness literature describes an interesting phenomenon called "The Commuting Paradox" that directly addresses this assumption.[4] As researchers have discovered, people with long commutes are, on average, less happy. This Commute Paradox phenomenon is quite consistent and demonstrates the tradeoff between time on the road and the happiness brought about by houses, schools, and pay does not work in the way most assume.

It seems illogical people would fight long commutes every day when the evidence shows they don't achieve the happiness they assume. Frankly, though, we all take actions assuming those actions lead to greater happiness when they don't. We stretch our finances with debt just to have the new luxury car we assume will make us happier. We spend long, grueling hours at work in anticipation of getting the promotion we think will make us happier. Fighting long commutes to provide for family is commendable, luxury cars are nice, and striving for a promotion is an admirable goal; however, none of these things bring lasting happiness. If they don't bring happiness, why do we assume they will? Frankly, society, family, and peers have delivered this message throughout our lifetimes. Because the message is so strong, I have had countless people argue they know they would be happier with more money. I like to ask them these probing questions:

- What income will bring you happiness? Is it $80,000 or $150,000 or $500,000 or $1,000,000?

- Have you ever met an unhappy millionaire?

- What day of the week do you think you'll reach the point of happiness? Will you wake up on a Tuesday morning after getting a big raise and discover you have now arrived at the point of lasting happiness?

These questions are obviously tongue-in-cheek, but I ask them to make a point. Happiness is not a time in the future where you arrive one day, and happiness is not based in "things."

If you pursue happiness by chasing "things," you might achieve certain goals and even moments of joy, but you will unfortunately not achieve sustained happiness. Simply stated, chasing "stuff" is not the path to happiness, but if you are like most people, you tell yourself your lack of happiness is due to not achieving enough. You must chase even more. You might think to be happier you just need to get to that next income level, or attain a certain level of wealth, achieve a higher health goal, buy an even bigger house, or get an even nicer car. Simply stated, chasing these types of goals does not provide a path to happiness. It is fine to pursue these things; just don't assume this is the path to happiness.

You have heard the phrase, "I will be happier when," and I would not be surprised if you have used it yourself. You might have said you will be happier when you:

- Lose weight.
- Are out of debt.
- Make $100,000 a year.
- Are no longer sick.

I have had the good fortune of speaking to audiences of various ages from high school students to retirees. I specifically recall working with a group of college seniors and asking the question, "What would make you happier?" Answers I heard from those college seniors included:

- I will be happier when I get a job.
- I will be happier when I get a car that is dependable.
- I will be happier when I buy a house.
- I will be happier when I get married.
- I will be happier when I start a family.

For contrast, I also recall a group of retirees, and their responses were a bit different:

- I will be happier when I fix my financial problems.
- I will be happier when I can walk without pain.
- I will be happier when I move near my grandchildren.

The specific answers may be different, but the sentiment remains the same. These individuals all assumed greater happiness was at a point in the future and would result from an event or set of events.

The great happiness researcher, Sonja Lyubomirsky, in her wonderful book, *The Myths of Happiness*,[5] describes how people will exaggerate certain future events, both positive and negative. According to Lyubomirsky, people tend to exaggerate how good that new car, new house, more money, or even seeing grandchildren will make them feel. These things indeed do bring wonderful moments of joy and even elation, but they do not provide long-term happiness.

Not only might you exaggerate the impact of future events; you likely also have flawed memories about past events. In Daniel Gilbert's seminal book, *Stumbling on Happiness*,[6] he describes how we all try to repeat experiences that brought us good feelings and how we try to avoid experiences that brought us displeasure or embarrassment. The problem, as he notes, is that our memories are flawed and therefore are not always a good basis for making decisions about the future.

"Memory is not a dutiful scribe that keeps a complete transcript of our experiences, but a sophisticated editor that clips and saves key elements of an experience and then uses these elements to rewrite the story each time we ask to reread it.... (A)s keen as its editorial skills may be, memory does have a few quirks that cause it to misrepresent the past and hence causes us to misimagine the future." [7]

Gilbert's observations can help you understand why you may be bad at predicting how certain experiences will make you feel in the future and therefore how you might not accurately predict your own happiness. The problem is you do not remember all experiences equally. You tend to remember the extreme or unusual occurrences and do not recall as vividly the mundane or ordinary occurrences.

This exaggeration does not only happen with negative events, it also happens with positive experiences. You might remember that time you took your children to Disney and saw their faces light up when they first walked down Main Street, and your mind thinks of this as a typical family vacation.

Unfortunately, when you predict future events, you rely on your memories, your flawed memories, to predict how you will feel. You tend to exaggerate the positive feelings that would come from buying a new house, and you also exaggerate the negative feelings that would come from losing your job. In summary, your memory tells you what will bring happiness, so you head down that path, but as I have now said repeatedly, it is not the path to happiness.

CHAPTER 3

HEDONIC ADAPTATION

You cannot accurately predict what will make you happy because you rely on flawed memories to predict the feelings of future events. Another psychological phenomenon, called Hedonic Adaptation, is also responsible for your inability to predict happiness. Have you ever felt thrilled after buying a new car? It was so beautiful and shiny, and it even smelled good. You might even remember those times you parked it and as you were walking away, you turned around and looked at it with adoration. But fast forward a few months. You were running out the door to go to work. You jumped in your car, which was so dirty someone could write "wash me" on the back, and it smelled like the pizza you carried home last night. It had extra jackets, umbrellas, and food wrappers strewn about, and it even had some fries that fell between the driver's seat and the center console. It was still that same wonderful car you bought and admired a few months before, but it was now just your car, a means of transporting you from one place to another. This psychological adjustment of how you felt about your car is an example of hedonic adaptation.

The term "hedonic" describes the feeling, typically a positive feeling, brought about by a thing or an event. It might be what you felt when you first walked into your new house or when you first heard you got that big promotion or when you danced at your wedding reception. These are very real feelings. They are wonderful, and they can be quite intense.

Such feelings can easily explain the previous illustration that assumed cars, vacations, and houses can lead from being unhappy to having lasting happiness. The combination of a faulty memory and hedonic adaptation can lead to these assumptions. Recall that your memory tends to recall more extreme feelings. Therefore, when you recall buying a car, taking a trip, or buying a house, you tend to recall the early, extreme feelings, and you are not as likely to recall the "adaptation" part of the events. You do not focus on the fact that your car just became another mode of transportation, that the trip was good, but you were very ready to wash the sand out of your clothes and sleep in your own bed, or that your house became a place that needed cleaning and a new air conditioning unit. Because you recall the more extreme positive feelings, you are also more likely to work every day to get those feelings again. Unfortunately, though, heading down that path can put you into a loop, which we call the Hedonic Treadmill, where you chase those things that can bring you such wonderful feelings, but you then adapt and want more.

Remember the term is Hedonic Adaptation, and adaptation is a key element to this equation. Simply stated, your feelings adapt to any good occurrence or sad occurrence. Research has shown that even lottery winners adapt to the big win. On the other side, adaptation can be beneficial, because you can have a terrible event and "adapt" to the negative impact of that event. For example, research has shown that people who have been in an accident and lost use of their legs eventually adapted to this new reality and returned to the same level of happiness they had before the accident.

Let's now go back to the unusual question I asked previously: Which of the following events would make you happier? (a) Breaking your leg or (b) Spending a week on the Greek Island of Santorini. The primary focus of this question was which would make you happier, not which one you would choose. I promised you I would return to this unusual question and give you the answer. Here it is:

The answer is: NEITHER!

It may seem difficult to believe, but one of these events will not bring you more lasting happiness than the other. Research shows regardless of which answer you choose, in about 18-24 months you will return to the level of happiness you had before you made the decision.[8] You might find it surprising to learn the negative event might even bring you a little more happiness than going to Santorini.

I am reminded of a time years ago when I gave a graduation speech in which I asked if winning the lottery or getting a diagnosis of a serious illness would make you happier. I explained that the human mind tends to adapt to life events and neither event would bring more lasting happiness than the other. I also said that, in fact, the diagnosis might bring a little more happiness because it could yield a new perspective on life. The next morning, a woman walked up to me as I was getting out of my car, and she said, "Dr. Harmon, you don't know me, but I heard you speak at graduation yesterday." She then went on to say some kind and complimentary things about the speech. As she continued, she said something that truly struck me, "When you asked the question about the illness or the lottery, I could identify. Just over a year ago, my husband was diagnosed with cancer. Thankfully, he recently received wonderful news and is in remission, but I can tell you after he received that diagnosis, we lived life to the fullest. His diagnosis gave us perspective, and we now embrace every day and are happier than ever." By this time, she had started to shed some tears, and I will admit those tears were contagious. She was so generous to share her thoughts and emotions with me. I never got her name, but she illustrated the point better than I ever could.

You might think it a shame we adapt to life events. After all, wouldn't it be wonderful if every positive life event took you to a new level of happiness? That sounds good initially but remember there is a positive element to this adaptation. When you have negative events in life, sometimes even traumatic experiences, your mind can do amazing things by helping you adapt. This does not mean the negative experiences cannot have deep, lasting scars. They certainly can, but the scars are often not as deep or lasting because of hedonic adaptation.

Understanding hedonic adaptation can give you a newfound strength in your daily life. While I would not want your life to have negative experiences, your new knowledge about hedonic adaptation can help you adapt and keep you from worrying as much. You also can start to realize that external events, which are often term life circumstances, are not the key to your happiness or to your unhappiness. Instead, your happiness is determined somewhere else.

CHAPTER 4

THE ARRIVAL FALLACY[9]

Understanding hedonic adaptation is key to understanding happiness. Assume you are hoping to become a partner at a large law firm. In your mind, becoming a partner will completely change your life. You will have greater financial compensation, enhanced job security, and increased professional prestige. You have had this goal ever since you graduated law school. You always imagined becoming a partner would give you a better life and a happier life. Then the day arrives when you become a partner. It is a wonderful day. Everyone is celebrating, and you are already thinking about putting in that pool or taking that exotic trip next year.

Months pass by, and you get accustomed to your new lifestyle, and eventually you experience hedonic adaptation. The "newness" wears off and the excitement fades. But you might experience even more negative feelings than those simply explained by hedonic adaptation. You might experience something known as the Arrival Fallacy.

Dr. Tal Ben-Shahar coined the term, "The Arrival Fallacy,"[10] to describe the emptiness that can follow once you achieve a significant goal. This feeling is logically linked to hedonic adaptation, but it goes beyond the lessening of excitement following achievement of a goal; it describes more extreme empty, negative feelings that can follow goal attainment. The Arrival Fallacy is a phenomenon even more negative than hedonic adaptation. You might achieve a goal, often a significant goal, and then have a lack of purpose and a sense of being unsatisfied afterward. The process of pursuing the goal is exhilarating and exciting and creates a daily sense of optimism. Once you achieve the goal, though, these positive emotions can vanish, and you can go into a lull.

There are at least two reasons you might feel this lull after attaining a goal. You previously saw a goal, chased it, and then achieved it. However, after achieving it, there was no longer "the chase." You no longer had the excitement of imagining the endless possibilities this new goal would bring.

Just by being human, you are naturally driven toward goals, and many psychological theories explain this drive. You can even go back to Maslow, who posited that human beings have a constant drive to better themselves and, eventually, arrive at self-actualization.[11]

You are naturally driven to pursue goals, and that pursuit can be fun and even exhilarating. The path of pursuit generates feelings of anticipation and optimism about how life will look once you arrive at your goal. The exhilaration can fade, though, once your goal is achieved.

There is another reason you might feel an emotional lull once you arrive at a goal. Simply stated, the goal might not bring the same joy you imagined. Recall the example of becoming a partner at your law firm. You were pursuing that goal and imagining how wonderful life would be with your new salary and new prestige. You would be able to build the new pool, your financial stress would be gone, and you would have a much higher profile at work and in the community.

You might imagine similar scenarios with other goals. For example, you might imagine the bliss of living with the love of your life after your big wedding day that you planned for so long. Or soon after learning you are pregnant, you might imagine the joy of a baby's first giggles and watching your child grow up. These are delightful goals and even extraordinary experiences, but the level of happiness they bring may not be at the level you expected.

I have been in higher education for most of my career and have held leadership positions at five universities. Individuals often came to me asking for advice, saying "I want to be a dean" or "I want to be a provost" or "I want to be a president." We would have lengthy talks about how they could pursue these positions, but I would inevitably ask them one simple question: "Why?" I was curious what they imagined the new position would bring to their lives and why they wanted to pursue such a goal.

Their answers varied but usually included lofty, altruistic goals about making a difference, enhancing culture, or mentoring others. I loved these answers, but inevitably I talked to them a little more and discovered they had other motivations, as well, such as money, prestige, or authority. They had altruistic objectives, but they also were human and anticipated great joy and happiness from the things such a position would bring.

I enjoyed watching many of these individuals achieve their desired positions, and I of course celebrated their accomplishments. But I also found it interesting to talk to them after they had been in the new position for a few months. They were satisfied with their positions, but they typically expressed frustrations and realizations that the position was not what they imagined. It might involve more hours or more headaches or more conflict than they imagined. The additional salary was nice (and I might even see the nice new car in the parking lot), but it was apparent hedonic adaptation was starting to set in, and they might even be experiencing what Dr. Ben-Shahar termed the Arrival Fallacy, where the new position might not be everything they imagined. I am not saying they regretted chasing their leadership positions; that was rarely the case. They were content, but it was apparent they did not feel the same optimism and drive they had before they attained their positions. The chase was over, and the result was not as enthralling as they imagined.

You might think experiencing hedonic adaptation or the Arrival Fallacy would cause people to temper their enthusiasm for chasing goals such as salaries and positions. They consciously know they adapt and might even feel disappointment with their accomplishment. Yes, you might think people would "learn" from past experiences. However, quite the opposite is true. People get back on the Hedonic Treadmill, chase the next goal, and never arrive at their desired level of happiness.

Why would you keep getting back into that loop of chasing the next goal thinking it will bring you greater happiness? The reason is that your conscious mind is not the key player in this scenario. Your subconscious mind runs your life and "tells" you what to focus on. It is your subconscious mind that has the faulty memory, remembers the bigger emotions from the past, recalls the times before hedonic adaptation set in, and forgets the disappointment you felt after achieving your previous goal. Therefore, in order to understand the happiness lessons more fully, you need to learn a little more about your subconscious and the way your brain works.

CHAPTER 5

THE HAPPINESS PERCENTAGE

I assume you have very definite ideas about what makes you happy. I previously shared ideas people mentioned during my speeches, such as family, music, travel, reading a book, their dog, and friends. As you reflect on your own list of what makes you happy, I imagine it feels good and brings you joy to reflect on your own experiences. And because you have such fond memories, your subconscious is pushing you to pursue those things again. I agree with your subconscious. You should pursue those things on your list. After all, such moments are quite special, should be celebrated, and contribute to a meaningful life. But I am also warning you not to assume the pursuit will bring you lasting happiness.

At this point in the book, I need to admit I have not been completely honest. I need to be more precise when I say the things on your list do not bring happiness. According to happiness research, pursuing the things on your list can indeed increase your happiness. But I warn you the increase is not very large and does not make a substantial difference in your life.

I once was delivering a happiness speech to a large group and again asked the audience members to list three things that make them happy and list three things that would make them happier. As they started to respond, I grabbed a marker and wrote down each response on a board in front of the room.

I soon had a large list that included many things I had heard before, such as family, dogs, music, children, grandchildren, the beach, and reading a book. However, this group started to have fun with the list and were feeding off one another. The list grew larger and the items on the list became more extreme. They were having a great time, as was I, so they kept calling out ideas, and I kept writing. Their list looked like this:

Salary	Wealth	Family	Children
Grandchildren	Health	Nice Car	Vacations
Nice Clothes	Days on the Beach	Time with Friends	Reading Books
Exercise	Yoga	Massages	Getting Married
Winning $30 million	A Dog	Beach House in Europe	Private Jet

I wanted to drive home the idea that even this list brings only a limited amount of happiness. To do so, I turned the list into the following equation and asked them how much all of these things, in total, would contribute to their happiness:

Salary + Wealth + Family + Children + Grandchildren + Health + Nice Car + Vacations + Nice Clothes + Days on the Beach + Friends + Reading Books + Exercise + Yoga + Massages + Getting Married + Winning $30 Million in the Lottery + Dog + Beach House in Europe + Private Jet = _____% of Your Happiness

They started debating the percentage. Some were saying it had to be close to 100% because this would be a wonderful life. I agreed with them that it looked amazing. After all, you could put your family and dog and friends on your private jet and read a book while jetting to your beach house in Italy.

But then I had to bring them back to reality and said we needed to look at the happiness research to determine the percentage. In fact, the research is clear. If you had all the items on this list, the TOTAL effect on your overall happiness would be only 10%.[12]

When I reveal this percentage to audiences, I typically hear a large, collective gasp. They imagine jets and wealth and multiple homes. They assume this lifestyle would affect their happiness by more, much more, than 10%. How could the percentage be so low? Look at that list! That looks like a truly grand life, but hedonic adaptation does not discriminate. Yes, you even adapt to the jet and the Italian villa.

Your subconscious assumes the percentage is higher, which also explains why you might watch television shows about the rich and famous. You imagine how amazing their lives must be and how much happier you would be if you were rich and famous like them. On those days when you are scrambling, fighting traffic, feeling frustrated at work, and wondering how you are going to pay for your child's dance lessons, it is important to know all these struggles also contribute to only 10% of your happiness, or in this case, your unhappiness. And when you are envious of someone who just won the lottery or someone you see disembarking from their private jet, remember the 10% number and realize they might be much less happy than you.

Please don't think I am saying the things on this list are bad. Not at all! I love a day at the beach, playing my guitar, having dinner with friends, a great bottle of Bordeaux, or eating Memphis ribs (I had to say it). I will also admit I have had the great fortune to have rides on private jets with my generous friends, and it is an incredible way to travel. Yes, I enjoy, or would enjoy, the things on the list. For those things I can actually achieve, I enjoy them in the moment and reflect fondly on them afterward. They provide beautiful moments and memories, but I also know they do not create enduring happiness.

Let's explore this 10% even more. Recall my previous quote: "Most people wake up every day and work against their own happiness." The primary reason this quote is true is because most people believe "the happiness percentage" is much higher than it is and therefore chase those externalities with great vigor. They wake up every day and fight like crazy to achieve the next goal or get the money for the family vacation, and while going down this path toward what they think is happiness, they fail to realize they are only chasing a maximum of 10%. They usually don't even realize there is a much greater path, the path to true happiness.

I have used the term "externalities" to explain those external factors you tend to chase every day. Researchers use a better, more inclusive, term when discussing the 10%. They use the term "life circumstances." I like this term, because it goes beyond things you chase on a given day and includes all the things in your life, including those out of your control. If you remember "life circumstances" contribute only 10% of your happiness, then you will be less likely to say, "I can't be happy because I have had some real financial struggles" or "I can't be happy because I went through a nasty divorce" or "I can't be happy because my son and his family moved out of state." You may not feel elated during these tough times, but they only affect your long-term happiness by 10%.

It's time to explore the other 90% and understand what you can control. This understanding will help support the five Happiness Lessons later in this book. If life circumstances only contribute to 10% of your happiness, then the next logical question is whether you can control the other 90%. You cannot control all the 90%, but you can control much of it, enough to make an enormous difference in your life.

Psychology research shows you have a genetic, natural predisposition to a certain level of happiness, which we often term your "happiness setpoint." You might be born to be incredibly happy, moderately happy, or even less happy. I tend to call this setpoint your "happiness thermostat," because much like a thermostat, it works to bring you back to your predetermined level of happiness, just as a thermostat will control the room temperature. You can have amazing life events, such as winning the lottery, or even terrible life events, such as a divorce, but either way, your happiness will tend to move back toward its happiness setpoint.[13]

Hearing about this genetic predisposition, you might be inclined to use it as an excuse not to work on your happiness, and you might even say, "This is how I was born. I'm going to be unhappy and there is nothing I can do about it." The truth is there is something you can do about it, so it is time to understand a bit more about the setpoint. The good news is this set point, or thermostat, contributes to approximately 50% of your happiness. Turning back to math, if you recall that life circumstances contribute to 10% of your happiness and you know that 50% of your happiness is set by your genetics, this explains approximately 60% of your happiness, which leaves 40%. The great news is you can adjust this 40% through your own actions. The five Lessons in Section 3 teach you exactly how you can adjust the 40%.

CHAPTER 6

THOSE HAPPINESS
RANKINGS DON'T HELP

Before we introduce the happiness lessons, it's important to reflect on something that is well-intentioned but can pull you away from sticking to the happiness lessons: The Happiness Rankings. Because I am known to many people as "The Happiness Guy," I often receive messages referring to the latest "List of the Happiest _____" where you can fill in the blank with Cities, States, Countries, Jobs, etc. These rankings are fun to read, but they imply that if you were to move to a specific location or get a particular job, you would become happier.

These lists get considerable attention. After all, aren't you always looking for greater happiness? When you see San Diego or Hawaii on the list of happiest places, you might imagine yourself in one of those settings and you just "know" you would be happier if you were there. You imagine yourself waking up every morning breathing in the fresh air near the shores of La Jolla or Hanauma Bay. After seeing such a list, you might sigh and say, "Wouldn't it be wonderful to live there? I know why people there are so happy."

Since you crave happiness, as everyone does, you gravitate toward articles about happiness rankings, and you imagine how much happier you would be "if." You see a lot of these articles about lists, because the authors know you crave more happiness. The authors are not sinister in their motives; they are promoting happiness by getting you to think about it and talk about it. Admittedly, the lists are fun to explore, but they have a negative side. They unfortunately could be contributing to your misunderstanding of happiness and could cause you to continue chasing those "life circumstances" in the 10% category.

I have been promoting happiness for many years, so when I think of "the happiest city" or the "happiest country," I automatically think of a place with the greatest percentage of happy people. And when I picture a place with a large percentage of happy people, it sounds delightful and sounds like a place I would want to live. Unfortunately, most of these rankings do not measure the percentage of happy people. In fact, they usually do not measure happiness at all. Instead, they typically measure things that "should" make you happy. Here are a few examples of measures used in developing some recent happiness rankings: [14]

- GDP per capita
- Social support
- Healthy life expectancy
- Freedom to make life choices
- Generosity
- Perceptions of corruption
- Depression rate
- Suicide rate
- Physical health
- Life expectancy

- Share of adults feeling "productive"
- Adequate sleep rate
- Sports participation
- Food insecurity
- Income-growth rate
- Unemployment rate
- Job satisfaction
- Commute time
- Poverty rate
- Number of work hours
- Economic mobility
- Job security
- Divorce rate
- Strength of social ties
- Volunteer rate
- Weather
- Parks per capita
- Ideal weather days
- Community engagement
- Crime rates

These are very positive traits, and I can see why they would make a place desirable. The problem is the methodology is supposed to be measuring happiness, not desirable traits. These desirable traits are in the category of life circumstances and therefore contribute to only 10% of your happiness.

When you read these lists, do you ever wonder, "If I were to move to that place, would I become happier?" For example, if you are unhappy and you move to Finland (always a high achiever on the happiness scale),[15] would you change from being unhappy to happy just based on your location?

Based on what you now know about the happiness percentage, you realize the answer is "No."

I am reminded of an old parable that highlights this very well. According to the parable, an old lady was sitting by the side of a road that led to a small village. A man was walking on the road toward the village, and he stopped to talk to the old lady: "Hello. I am moving to this village. Do you know how the people are? Are they friendly? Are they fun?" The old lady asked him a question: "How were the people in the village you are coming from?" The man responded, "Oh, they were wonderful. I had many friends there, and everyone was fun and friendly." The lady responded, "I am certain you will find the people in this village to be the same."

A little while later, another man was walking down the same road toward the village, saw the old lady, and stopped to talk: "Hello. I am moving to this village. Do you know how the people are? Are they friendly? Are they fun?" The old lady asked him the same question she asked the previous man: "How were the people in the village you are coming from?" This man responded, "They were the worst. They were grumpy and unfriendly. I could not wait to get out of there." The old lady responded, "Unfortunately, I think you will find the people in this village to be the same."

This parable has always stuck with me, and I think it captures the essence of the happiness research. If you drop a happy person into a new place, they will still be a happy person. If you drop an unhappy person into a new place, they will still be unhappy. Of course, if the unhappy person wants to become happier, they can take deliberate steps to become happier, regardless of where they are.

Back to the happiness lists. They are fun, but they unfortunately reinforce a misconception that external factors such as income equality, access to healthcare, etc. will bring you happiness. You picture Hawaii, imagine beautiful weather and lovely ocean breezes, and then assume living in Hawaii would bring you greater happiness. In a recent report, the next two states after Hawaii were Maryland and New Jersey.[16] I have nothing against Maryland or New Jersey and have had wonderful times in both, but I doubt they conjure the same images as Hawaii. I like to say the happiest state you can live in is your own state of mind. We now can learn how you can adjust your state of mind and become happier.

SECTION 2

WHAT TRULY MAKES YOU HAPPY

*"Happiness is a Choice,
Not a Result"*
-RALPH MARSTON[17]

CHAPTER 7

BECOMING A GREAT DRUMMER

You now have a good idea of what doesn't make you happy, but I'm guessing that's not why you picked up this book. To understand the importance of the happiness lessons presented in Section 3, though, you must put "things" and "life circumstances" into perspective and realize they only contribute to 10% of your happiness. You should enjoy days at the beach, new cars, and even jets and vacation homes, but the important lesson is that, because of hedonic adaptation, those good feelings are fleeting, and you soon revert to your happiness setpoint. Simply stated, things and life circumstances do not provide the path to happiness.

You next logical question might be, "If those things don't make me happy, what does?" This is a perfectly appropriate question, and the answers are coming soon. We are getting to the really fun part of this book, but first you need to understand how your brain works.

Assume you want to be a great drummer, a truly great drummer. You want to be recognized with such notable drummers as Neil Peart, John Bonham, Keith Moon (sorry, my nostalgic old rock roots are showing), Carter Beauford, Stewart Copeland, or even my new-found favorite, El Estepario Siberiano. You have decided you want to be world famous for your skills as a drummer.

Just deciding you want to be a great drummer is not sufficient. You might have natural skills and talent, but even if you have natural talent, you must hone that talent to be truly great. Honing your talent requires you to receive guidance and lessons from someone who knows the path to being a great drummer. You need a teacher who can give you lessons. You then need to practice those lessons, and in order to improve, you will need to be very deliberate and practice the lessons every day.

I had a guitar instructor in Arizona who was an amazing player, excelling in both rock guitar and classical guitar, and he was successful in the Phoenix music scene. I would sit in awe as he would play so beautifully and effortlessly. One day during a lesson, we were discussing the importance of practice, and he told me he practiced at least three hours every day. Three hours? Every day? I was envious of his discipline and dedication, but I also wondered why he felt the need to practice so much. After all, he was already an outstanding guitar player. His explanation was that he wanted to hold onto his skills and wanted to get even better, which meant he needed to practice every day.

You may think I've lost my mind (a separate issue) discussing drummers and guitar players. You are supposed to be learning about happiness, and I am going on and on about being a great drummer or a great guitarist. Frankly, the same rules apply if you want to be a great drummer, guitar player, tennis player, golfer, speaker, race car driver, or a happier person. You must learn lessons and practice the lessons every day.

Yes, the same process applies to happiness. If you want to have enduring happiness, you need to receive lessons about how to be happier and then practice those lessons every day. I hope you now realize the ultimate purpose of this book is to give you the lessons you can practice to make you happier. We will get there, but before you get to the actual lessons, it is important for you to understand what happens when you practice and why practice is so important. In other words, you must understand your subconscious mind.

CHAPTER 8

THE POWER OF
THE SUBCONSCIOUS MIND

Your subconscious mind is a powerful and important force in your life. It is primarily responsible for almost everything you do, and it even determines whether you are happy or unhappy.

Your mind has both a conscious component and a subconscious component. The conscious mind is that part of the mind you are aware of and helps you think about what you want to do today, where you want to go on vacation, or what you want for lunch. This part of the mind seems to control much of your life, so you accordingly give it prominence in your life's direction. For example, if you have a habit of running late for appointments, you might think you simply need to refocus your conscious mind on being on time. What you do not realize, though, is that your conscious mind is not the part of your brain controlling whether you're late. Your subconscious mind is in control of most things and is what is telling you that you are habitually late. Therefore, if you want to establish a habit of being on time, you must focus your efforts on retraining your subconscious mind.

When it comes to happiness, you might think, "I'm not as happy as I would like to be," and then tell yourself you need to focus your conscious mind on being happier. This is a great goal, but unfortunately, the conscious mind cannot get the job done by itself. Being happier takes an effort to retrain your subconscious mind, and that takes a combination of your conscious mind and subconscious mind.

It's important to understand the relative size and power of your conscious and subconscious mind. According to psychologists, the conscious mind occupies only 5% of your brain's capacity, and the other 95% is your subconscious mind. The subconscious mind is obviously more significant than the conscious. The subconscious tells you to breathe, blink, or sweat, and it tells you how to walk or drive a car. In other words, the subconscious mind runs virtually every part of your life.[18]

How does the subconscious mind get its information? It starts gathering information the moment you are born and you start to observe the world. Young children do not instinctively know that if they release a ball from their hand the ball will fall to the ground. However, once they observe the ball falling enough times, they realize the ball does, indeed, fall to the ground every time, and this fact becomes part of their subconscious. Have you ever noticed a young child will sometimes drop a ball, or your keys, repeatedly, often providing frustration in the process? Parents might attribute this behavior as the child being playful or even mischievous. Typically, though, the child is in the process of learning, or more accurately, training their subconscious mind.

Your subconscious continues learning as you have additional interactions with others and experience life events. If you have traumatic experiences in your childhood, your subconscious retains this information, and your future thoughts, actions, and even relationships are affected. Your negative experiences as a child can dictate your moods, your relation-ships, and even your life decisions 40 years later, even though you are not aware of the powerful influence those negative experiences continue to have.

Your subconscious is remarkably powerful and dictates how you interact with the world. Your subconscious was trained or "wired" by every interaction, event, success, failure, and person you have encountered in your life. Knowing this fact can make you feel helpless. You might think, "Well, I guess my subconscious is pretty well set and there is nothing I can do about it." It is this type of thinking that drives people to say things like:

"I tend to be late for everything. I just can't help it."

"I'm overweight; that's just who I am."

"I'm just not a happy person."

If you repeatedly tell yourself you're not a good drum-mer, then eventually your subconscious mind believes you, and you will not be a good drummer. Telling yourself you're a great drummer doesn't mean you will soon be a first-call studio player in Nashville. However, if you think you have potential, repeatedly affirm yourself, and take deliberate steps toward training your subconscious to be a great drummer, then you are on the way to being a good, and possibly great, drummer. You will undoubtedly be the best drummer you can be if you sufficiently incorporate your subconscious mind.

Remember the young child who absorbs new knowledge like a sponge and quickly trains their subconscious mind? That child might learn what happens when they drop the keys, but they also learn from other parts of their environ-ment and eventually learn positivity or negativity, and even happiness or unhappiness.

Have you ever known that person who always sees the negative side of things? I imagine you do. These people suffer from something I call "The Cold Green Beans Effect." Imagine you are having a wonderful lunch with your friend Sarah. You are meeting to catch up on life, and Sarah is sharing her various life tragedies, such as frustrations with her marriage, difficulties with her children, pressures at work. Just after the server brings your lunch, Sarah says, "I always liked this restaurant, but today my green beans are cold." You guessed it, Sarah suffers from The Cold Green Beans Effect.

If you were to reach over and taste Sarah's green beans, you might realize they are, indeed, cooler than you would like. But that is not the point of the lesson. The point of the lesson is that the green beans may be cold, but Sarah could just as easily have pointed out that the server was very pleasant, the chicken was absolutely delicious, or her water had just the right amount of ice. She did not focus on these more positive aspects, though, because Sarah has trained her subconscious mind over the years to focus on negative things around her. Unfortunately, she doesn't even realize it; her training has been slow and steady, and it started when she was young. Sadly, Sarah will be less happy in life, because that remarkably powerful force, her subconscious mind, is her telling her to find the negative things around her.

Your brain has connectors that help process your thoughts, and the brain loves efficiency. Therefore, if you tend to have negative thoughts, your brain will create connectors, or bridges, to help those thoughts process more efficiently. This means the more negative thoughts you have, the easier it is for you to have even more negative thoughts in the future.[19]

The subconscious mind is immensely powerful, controls virtually everything in your life, and has learned from everything you have encountered over the years. But rather than think you are doomed to whatever your subconscious mind has learned thus far, the good news is you can take deliberate actions toward retraining your subconscious mind. With adequate time and appropriate training, you can be on time for appointments, you can lose that weight, and yes, you can be happier.

CHAPTER 9

THE SUBCONSCIOUS
AND HAPPINESS

All three of my daughters play the piano, and I recall watching them when they were first learning. They would look at that sheet of music and recall the mnemonic, "Every Good Boy Does Fine" to remember the lines on the treble clef (E-G-B-D-F). They would place their fingers on the keyboard with thumb at middle C, look back and forth between the sheet music and the keyboard, and proceed cautiously and carefully.

What came out of the piano in those initial stages did not sound much like music. The girls were too focused on how to read the notes, where the notes were on the piano, and how to place their fingers. But they practiced and practiced and practiced. They practiced for months and then for years. Eventually, they no longer had to interpret the notes on the sheet of music or wonder where to place their fingers. These actions now came naturally and seemingly effortlessly.

They had shifted their playing from their conscious minds to their subconscious minds. Consistent practice retrained their subconscious minds, and, after a while, their subconscious minds took over. This same phenomenon is why when you first learn to drive a car, you are consciously thinking about every little action you need to take. After hours of driving practice, though, your subconscious takes over, and you can now jump in a car and drive with truly little conscious thought. In fact, you now can drive the car, eat a hamburger, dig for fries, and talk to your best friend all at the same time (although this is not recommended).

Consistent practice retrains your subconscious, and your subconscious drives your actions. After my girls dedicated considerable hours to practicing, their subconscious minds took over. They then could sit at the piano, look at the sheet music, and play effortlessly, and what came out of the piano was beautiful music. The difference between those first days of fumbling for the right keys and the days of effortlessly playing beautiful music can be described by one word: Practice!

How did practice make them better? They developed certain muscle memory in their hands and fingers, but more importantly, practice moved their playing from their conscious minds to their subconscious minds. In the initial stages, they would have to think consciously about what each note was, where that note was on the piano, and then which finger they should place on that note. In other words, their conscious mind was engaged. Eventually, though, the practice caused the subconscious mind to take over, and they could play instinctively.

Your subconscious is a powerful force that has been learning ever since you were born. It dictates your everyday actions and your attitudes and moods. It therefore controls your happiness. Recall the previous discussion about 90% versus 10%. Only 10% of your happiness is attributed to externalities or life circumstances. The other 90% is attributed to you. You might also remember that 50% of your mind is preset from your DNA and life experiences. However, the exciting news is you still have 40% of your subconscious that can be retrained. My daughters took piano lessons, practiced the lessons, and trained their subconscious minds. They could then play beautiful music without thinking consciously about the details. You can do the same with happiness. You can receive lessons, practice those lessons, and then be instinctively happier in your daily life. This book is your starting point and gives you the lessons.

CHAPTER 10

DO YOU REALLY
WANT TO BE HAPPIER?

If you're like most people, you don't understand your own happiness and even work against it daily. The good news is you now understand the power of your subconscious mind, so you are one step closer to your own happiness journey. Before you embark on that journey, you must answer one powerful question: Do you really want to be happier?

You might be thinking, "That's a stupid question. Of course I want to be happier!" But wanting to be happier is quite different than making the decision to take the necessary steps to be happier. Much like the earlier discussion about great drummers, you might want to be a great drummer, but are you willing to do the things it takes to be a great drummer?

I could similarly ask you the question, "Do you want to be healthier?" I expect your response to be, "Of course I want to be healthier." But are you willing to do the things necessary to be healthier? Are you willing to give up the chips and queso, take your supplements on a regular basis, and get to the gym at least three times a week? As with any life change, you need to make a commitment and stick to it. The good news is the happiness journey is much easier and more fun than giving up chips and queso (at least for me).

You must first decide it is time to take control of your life. My father, Bill Harmon ("Grandaddy Bill" to Ashley), would often tell me, "Life is not a dress rehearsal." He was telling me I should live the life I want, starting today. You will see a quote, attributed to Confucius, at the beginning of the next section saying, "We have two lives, and the second begins when we realize we only have one." It's a powerful reminder to live with intention, appreciating the present instead of postponing life for "someday." Once you truly internalize the fact that your time is limited, you can begin living a more fulfilling, and happier, life.

I assume you picked up this book because you want to be happier. You want to live a life filled with beauty and positivity. My advice is to take complete control of your life and steer it toward happiness. If you want to be happier, then be happier. It just takes commitment. In this case, though, the commitment is powerful and immediately rewarding.

Consider the story of Deborah (not her real name). A few years ago, I was Deborah's leadership coach. As I do with all my clients, I started by letting her know this is her life, not a dress rehearsal, and she had the power to be who she wanted to be. For the next couple of years, we worked toward visualizing who she wanted to be as a leader and how to get there. She was brilliant and a sponge, and she learned the lessons well and put them into practice each day.

But there was another side to Deborah's story. When I started working with Deborah, she was quite heavy and had some health issues. We never discussed her weight, but I could tell it bothered her. Once Deborah started taking control in her professional life, she similarly took control in her personal life and began a journey of transition. Deborah completely changed her diet, started exercising, and lost more than 100 pounds. I recently met with Deborah to catch up on life, and to this day (years later) Deborah looks absolutely amazing and happy. I do not want to minimize the difficulty of her journey, but it all started with the realization she had the power to be the person she wanted to be. I take no credit for her tremendous transformation. I simply planted a seed of self-determination; she made the decision, and she made the difficult journey.

Deborah's journey is much like yours. You must decide happiness is something you want to pursue, and you must work daily toward that goal. The happiness journey is admittedly easier than losing weight or getting fit, but it still requires dedication and tenacity.

Before we get to the five lessons, we must address one more topic: sadness. During the Q&A portion of my speeches, I frequently get the question, "Do you ever get sad?" Yes, of course I get sad, and I see sadness as an integral part of the happiness journey. As a human being, you have many emotions. You have happiness, but you also have anger, anxiety, embarrassment, fear, and sadness. Emotions are part of life. To me, they are a beautiful part of life, and I think you should embrace all your feelings, even sadness.

Happiness does not eliminate sadness; instead, it helps you cope with sadness. When you take control of your life, you also take control of your emotions, which means dealing with your emotions rather than burying them. As a psychologist friend once told me, "Ken, if you bury your emotions, you bury them alive. They will return." Buried emotions do indeed return, and they sometimes return in unexpected ways and can be quite damaging. The healthier approach is to recognize your sadness, feel your sadness, but also realize the sadness is only temporary.

Another analogy I frequently use is healing from a physical wound. Imagine you are in a terrible car accident, and you have a deep gash in your thigh, a large, deep cut that is quite painful and limits your mobility. Just after the crash, you are unable to walk. If you ignore the pain and go out for a run, you would create even more pain and do more damage. Rather than trying to run too soon, you need to know your leg is going to hurt, and it will be a long journey toward recovery. Feeling the pain is part of your recovery; however, with care, attention, and patience, you will recover and might run again. The same is true for emotions. You will have events in your life that bring sadness and pain. These events could include death of a loved one, divorce, injury, job loss, or financial difficulties. Ignoring the feelings that come with these events would be like trying to run after your leg injury. If you ignore the feelings, you could do even more damage. Instead, you should feel your feelings and know that with care, attention, and patience, you will come out on the other side as a happy, and possibly even happier, person.

This is where the exciting stuff begins! The next section contains five lessons to help you retrain your subconscious and make you happier. Consider again the notion of becoming a great drummer. You can't receive fundamental drum lessons and immediately play at an advanced level. Instead, you must practice, practice, practice. The same is true for happiness. Think of these lessons as practice drills. Be deliberate about your practice and practice every day. The research shows that with consistent practice you will be measurably happier in a short period of time.[20] My own experience tells me the initial increase in happiness is just the beginning of a beautiful experience, and your happiness increases as you continue to practice. Try to be consistent in your practice but be gentle with yourself. You will lag in your efforts and even regress at times. Such setbacks are normal and expected. Progress is not a straight line; it has ups and downs, but the trend is upward. You will have "up" days and "down" days, but remember you are increasing your happiness over the long run. Happiness is not a destination; it is in the journey itself. Happiness is in each moment.

I am very excited for you. I can candidly and emphatically say these lessons have changed my life. Even in times of great difficulty, I have found greater peace, and long-term happiness, than I ever could imagine.

Your life is about to change for the better. I promise!

Here we go! It's now time for you to be happier!

SECTION 3

THE HAPPINESS LESSONS

"We have two lives, and the second begins when we realize we only have one."

—CONFUCIUS[21]

START WITH LOVE

"Love the whole world as a mother loves her only child."
— BUDDHA [22]

It was a Wednesday night, and I was chatting with John (not his real name), an executive I had coached for years. We were having a personal conversation and then the subject turned to work. He was telling me how angry he was with his employee, Frank (also not his real name). John had a meeting scheduled with Frank the next morning to discuss a troubling issue. John told me, "Ken, I am trying to stay calm, but I might just walk into that meeting and fire Frank right away. He really made me angry." I had been coaching John for a while, so I had gained his confidence. Also, John always wanted me to be open and candid, so I responded, "If you really feel that way, you should reschedule the meeting. Until you can walk into that meeting with love, reschedule it."

I used the word "love" to be dramatic and to get John's attention. Was I really asking him to shift his emotion from being angry with Frank to loving Frank? Yes, but when I talk about love, I am saying he should treat Frank as a human being who deserves to be heard. I admit I intended the words to be shocking, but I wanted John to walk into that meeting and listen to Frank, see Frank's perspective, and even give Frank the benefit of the doubt. He needed to see Frank as a person, not an object of his anger. If he listened to John openly and honestly and he still thought John should be given other career opportunities, then so be it. When I was leaving that night, I wasn't sure which course John would take, and I looked forward to hearing how it all turned out. Would John reschedule the meeting with Frank, or would he walk in and fire Frank right away?

I also knew Frank, because I had coached him as well. Thursday afternoon I saw a call coming in from Frank. I answered it, and Frank said, "Ken, I had a meeting with John this morning. It went really well, and I got a raise." I had a big smile on my face, and at that point I knew John had started with love.

In much the same way I intended to shock John, I named this lesson, "Start with Love," because I wanted to shock you, too. The word "love" evokes many emotions and I am certain the word even makes some of you uncomfortable. But remember the name of the lesson is, "Start" with Love. This means we start each encounter with love, whether it is someone at work, someone at home, someone on the road, or someone in the grocery store. Inevitably when I give this lesson to groups, I will quickly get the question, "Everyone? I'm supposed to love everyone?" My response is short but certain, "Yes! Everyone!"

If you start each encounter with love, you completely shift your mental focus to one of caring, compassion, and understanding. These emotions allow you to meet each person "where they are." When you start with love, you are more likely to connect with the other person, hear what they have to say, and see their humanity.

In my various management roles over the years, I've unfortunately had numerous occasions to fire employees. I didn't enjoy firing anyone, but each time I knew it was something that had to be done for the good of the organization and for the other people in the organization. Some of the people I fired had angered me by their actions. They might have committed fraud or treated a fellow employee poorly. Even on those occasions, as I walked into the room to deliver the bad news, I made every attempt to start with love. Trust me, it made a difference by helping me remain calm and setting a tone for the meeting.

Starting with love seems like a simple lesson, and it is, but when practiced daily and deliberately, starting with love carries tremendous power. I cannot adequately express how much this simple lesson has helped me in all parts of my life. People deserve to be loved just because they are people, and you should make every effort to have a positive connection.

While it sounds good to love other people, you might be wondering what this has to do with your own, lasting happiness. Remember that if you want to be happier, you must retrain your subconscious to focus on the positive, beautiful, happy things around you. When you start with love, you are learning to see the human side of everyone and the beauty that exists within them. Over time, your subconscious will learn the lesson of starting with love. You will automatically see the beauty in each person without even trying.

START WITH LOVE
ASSIGNMENTS

1. Reflect on this lesson and ask yourself what "starting with love" means to you. For example, does it mean always trying to see the best in people or giving people the benefit of doubt? Make it personal to you.

2. Here is a difficult assignment: Starting with love on the road. This is undoubtedly one of the most difficult places to demonstrate love. Try to start with love and be patient when a driver cuts in front of you or is looking at their phone when the light turns green. I sometimes hear people say, "Well, I can be more patient if I see it's a young driver or an older person." Try using that same approach because it's a human being, and human beings have flaws.

3. Happiness with a Friend: Recruit a friend to go through this book at the same time you are, and as you get to a lesson, talk to that friend and discuss your thoughts and experiences. For this "start with love" lesson, talk to your friend about what it means to you, where you have used it, and where you find it particularly difficult to implement.

4. Try some of these "start with love" lessons for a few weeks and then write your observations in the space below. Write down times you successfully started with love and times you had difficulty. Recording your reflections will help reinforce your successes and identify areas where you might need a little more practice.

NOTES

STOP COMPLAINING

*"If you don't like something, change it. If you can't
change it, change your attitude. Don't complain."*

— MAYA ANGELOU[23]

The human relations and leadership expert, Dale Carnegie, provided the sage advice: "Never criticize, condemn, or
complain."[24] Carnegie's powerful lesson has made a profound
difference in my life, helping me understand and connect to
others, even when I disagreed with them. More importantly,
though, this lesson helped me be happier.

When Dale Carnegie first provided this directive
nearly 100 years ago, he was trying to convince leaders to
connect with their employees and meet them where they
are. A leader who criticizes or condemns puts up an emotional wall, which can cause a lack of understanding and
perspective. This lesson has served me well in my own
leadership roles and still guides much of my leadership
coaching. It helped me connect to others and undoubtedly increased my own happiness.

Perhaps the most difficult part of Carnegie's directive is "stop
complaining." Complaining is something we all do, and we all
do much more than we realize. Like other happiness lessons,
though, a little insight will reveal how this all-too-common

habit makes you less happy, is harmful to your health, and yet is relatively easy to overcome.

I frequently and emphatically tell people: "Stop Complaining. It will make you happier." The reaction I receive is predictable. People scoff at the thought of not complaining. They see complaining as a way to focus on faults or problems that need to be corrected. This is occasionally true, but research shows 75% of complaining is not to correct a wrong but is instead just for the sake of complaining.[25]

In a recent seminar, I was discussing the negative effects of complaining when during the Q&A portion, someone took the audience microphone and asked: "What about venting? My friend and I get together every few days just to vent. We talk about frustrations at work and frustrations in our personal lives. It seems to help us cope." This same individual then leaned into the microphone and softly asked, "Is that okay, or is it affecting our happiness?"

I understand why people feel the need to vent, but as I replied to the woman at the microphone, "Venting may be something that feels good at the time, but please understand that venting, which is complaining, makes you less happy. If you know it affects your happiness and you still want to continue, that's up to you. But you might want to consider a different approach where you and your friend focus on positive things to discuss." She grinned and said, "I thought you might say that."

I recently posted on social media describing the dangers and pitfalls of complaining and how complaining makes you less happy. A good friend of mine quickly posted a comment and admonished me for this advice. She was upset that I would tell people not to complain. She demanded I consider the countless injustices in the world and said we all should "speak truth to power." As she further elaborated, "We must complain to bring real change to the world."

More recently, I attended a reception and a gentleman walked up, introduced himself, and said, "You look familiar." We started chatting, trying to remember where we had a previous connection. He finally exclaimed, "You're that happiness guy." I smiled and said I was, and he continued, "I liked what you said at the speech to our club, but I have a real disagreement with you. You told us to stop complaining. We all must complain, or else things wouldn't get better." He even gave the example of how a lawyer must file a "complaint" with a court. My response to my friend on social media and the gentleman at the reception was that they and I were talking about two different things. Highlighting an injustice or a wrong in order to correct the wrong is indeed necessary. I was referencing situations where the goal is just to complain, much like the woman talking about venting sessions with her friend. And as I noted previously, 75% of complaining is just for the sake of complaining.

Let's explore what is meant by "complaining." It may seem unusual to need explanation; after all, complaining is something we all do, and unfortunately do it quite frequently. Just like those two individuals who took me to task, you might think you complain in order to correct something, or to right an injustice. Unfortunately, though, these are not the typical reasons you complain. There is a strong distinction between complaining and stating a fact.

In his impactful book, *A Complaint Free World*, Will Bowen points out the difference between stating a fact and complaining.[26] He notes the distinction is in the energy expressed. For example, if I were to wake up on a Monday morning and calmly state, "It's raining," I have not necessarily made a complaint. I might be making a simple statement of fact about the weather, and this information might be useful when preparing for the day.

If I, instead, were to wake up on that same rainy Monday, let out a big sigh, and with exasperation say, "Oh no, it's raining" or "I can't believe it's raining," then I would be complaining. In this case, there is not the intent to relay useful information; there is the intent to voice displeasure about an event, not to correct it. After all, I can't do anything about the weather.

So, why do we complain? If there is no obvious beneficial outcome, why would we go to the trouble of complaining? The truth is we all have a desired outcome that is seen as beneficial, but it is typically part of our subconscious. The desired outcome is not to provide necessary information or to correct a wrong; the desired outcome is instead to receive attention or compassion from those around us. So, why do we have this desire and where did it start?

For most of us, it started when we were young children. Remember those times as a child when you didn't feel well? Maybe you had a fever or an upset stomach. What did you do on those occasions? That's right, you complained. At that young age you were not aware of the nuanced difference between stating a fact and complaining, so you expressed displeasure, or moaned, or whimpered, which are all just different forms of complaining. What happened next? You received care and compassion. Someone came running to take care of you, put a damp cloth on your head, tucked you in bed, brought you soup, and checked on you repeatedly. And on top of all that, you sometimes got to stay home from school and watch cartoons. You felt loved and comforted. What a wonderful outcome that started with the simple act of complaining.

As you grew older, you continued to complain. If you complained about the weather, your seat on the airplane, or the fact they forgot to put a pickle on your hamburger, did you expect someone to come comfort you? In a word, yes! You subconsciously desired compassion and empathy from others. You wanted them to have sympathy for your injustice, even if that injustice was only a pickle. Let's say you did get some sympathy or support when you complained about the pickle. Even though you achieved the result your subconscious wanted, you also had a negative result: you made yourself less happy.

Every time you complain, even if it's a small complaint, you make yourself a little less happy. As Bowen eloquently states it, "Complaining never attracts what you want; it perpetuates what you don't want."[27] He goes on to provide additional insight into complaining versus stating a fact. He asserts that complaining contains negative energy and is often a declaration of a perceived injustice. He then has a wonderful list of phrases that often accompany a complaint, thereby making it a complaint rather than a statement of fact:

"Of course!"

"Wouldn't you know it?"

"Just my luck!"

"This always happens to me!"

"Can you believe it?"

"No one cares about..."

"Here they go again!"[28]

This type of complaining is simply complaining to complain. You have no desire to correct a situation with this type of complaining; you just have the desire to complain and possibly receive sympathy. But let's be honest, sometimes it feels good to complain. In fact, I often have people argue with me: "Ken, I actually like to complain sometimes. It makes me feel better to get it out." I then respond with an analogy, perhaps an overly dramatic analogy, but it makes the point. When people tell me they feel better when they complain, I respond that I have known drug addicts who say how good they feel when that initial "hit" kicks in from the drug. This euphoric feeling keeps them coming back to the drug again and again, until it becomes a habit, and this habit can be very damaging to their health. Admittedly, comparing drug use to complaining may be overly dramatic, but the point is appropriate. You might feel good when you complain, but in the long run, complaining becomes a habit that can be very damaging to your health...and to your happiness.

In a recent article, "How Complaining Rewires Your Brain for Negativity,"[29] Dr. Travis Bradberry outlines interesting, and even startling, facts about complaining:

- In a typical conversation, most people complain at least once per minute.
- With continued complaining, the brain builds "bridges" to make it easier to complain.
- Complaining releases cortisol, the stress hormone, that can raise your blood pressure, raise your blood sugar, and impair your immune system.
- Complaining can make you more vulnerable to high blood pressure, diabetes, heart attack, and obesity.

- Complaining can shrink your hippocampus, which is responsible for problem solving and intelligent thought. [30]

These research results show complaining is a powerful, yet negative, force that can cause real health problems. Unfortunately, there is a "snowball" effect with complaining. The more you complain, the easier it is for you to complain, and therefore the cycle toward additional complaining continues.

Dr. Bradberry describes another interesting fact about complaining. The more you are around other people who complain, then their complaining can affect your health. It is much like smoking. If you smoke, it certainly affects your health; however, being around another person who smokes can also negatively impact your health. The same is true if you are around someone else who is a habitual complainer.

Complaining can negatively affect your health and can make you less happy. The more you complain, the more your subconscious becomes focused on negativity and is habitually scanning the environment for negative things to complain about. This is why complaining makes you less happy. Happiness is about seeing the good in the world and finding beauty around you. The more your subconscious is telling you to find negative things to complain about, it starts to block out your ability to intrinsically find beauty and positivity.

You now understand the harmful effects of complaining. You also have seen research that says with more complaining your brain will make it easier to complain. You need to learn how to shut off this cycle, complain less, and become happier.

The first lesson in shutting off the complaining cycle is

to recognize when you are complaining, deliberately catch yourself, and force yourself to stop. This sounds simple, but it takes focused and repeated effort. Your subconscious has learned unhealthy habits about complaining over many years, and it will take time and repeated effort to retrain your subconscious to instead focus on positivity.

Here are two techniques I have found helpful to stop complaining. First, you must make yourself aware you are, indeed, complaining. In his book, *A Complaint Free World*,[31] Bowen describes how he hands out bracelets to help stop complaining. His directive is that every time you complain, you should remove the bracelet from one wrist and switch it to the other wrist. This is a step beyond just catching yourself complaining. By using the physical activity of changing the bracelet from one wrist to the other, you are making a deeper connection to your subconscious. This process helps remind your subconscious not to find things to complain about and to therefore make it more difficult to complain.

The changing-wrist method also makes you aware just how much you are complaining. It can be interesting to set a goal, such as going one day without complaining. Trust me, it can be eye-opening to see how long you can go. And yes, going 24 hours without a single complaint seems virtually impossible.

Another method I have found effective is a version of something I call the "Shut-Up Technique." In my executive coaching, I frequently teach the Shut-Up Technique to help people shut down bad habits, such as worrying or complaining. The Shut-Up Technique can be an excellent first step toward taking control of your subconscious and steering your life toward greater happiness.

The Shut-Up Technique is quite simple. If you find yourself complaining, obsessing, or worrying too much, just tell yourself to shut up. I even advise you to say it out loud, because things you say out loud more easily reach your subconscious. I can candidly say I have used this technique countless times myself. I recall years ago I was walking through a grocery store in Murfreesboro, Tennessee, and I found myself in an endless loop of worrying about something going on in my life. I stopped in the middle of the grocery store aisle and, out loud, told myself, "Ken, shut up!" Thankfully, no other shoppers were on that aisle at the time, but it worked. It stopped my cycle of worry and helped me start to retrain my subconscious.

When it comes to complaining, there is only a slight adjustment in the wording of the Shut-Up Technique. I advise people to catch themselves complaining and then say, out loud if possible, "Stop it!" It is a way to remind your subconscious that you are the one in charge of your life.

There are a few more steps in the Stop-It Technique. Consciously telling yourself not to dwell on something or to stop complaining is a powerful way to start taking control of your subconscious. I have found it even more effective in asserting control, though, if you follow up by telling your subconscious exactly when and how you will focus on the issue.

Remember it is not good to bury your emotions, and if you have the compulsion to complain, you might feel you need to "let it out" and not bury it. I advise people to set a time to focus on the issue. Assume you are at work and find yourself frustrated and wanting to complain about your boss. To control this desire, you need to tell yourself two things.

First, you tell yourself to Stop It. At this point, it is helpful to remind yourself that complaining will make you less happy, even if your complaint is legitimate. After you tell yourself to Stop It, you then tell yourself you will focus on your boss's frustrating behavior at 6:00 that night. This follow-up statement, where you dictate when you will think about it, allows you to be in charge and also not bury your emotions. In effect, you are telling yourself, and your subconscious, you are not going to let life just happen to you. Your life is going to be yours to command.

In this scenario, when 6:00 p.m. rolls around, you must make the conscious decision of how you will address your frustrations with your boss. If there is something you can do about the situation, then use this time to write down what you would like to do or say. If, however, you just want to complain, one helpful technique is writing your frustrations on a sheet of paper, balling up the paper, and then throwing it away. Going through this physical process is more effective than just thinking about your frustrations. By writing your list of frustrations, you admit to yourself you have these emotions, but you also have the physical activity of balling up the paper and throwing it away, which tells your subconscious you are in charge.

STOP COMPLAINING
ASSIGNMENTS

1. The first step to stop complaining is to be aware you are complaining, even if you simply call it "venting." Unless you are trying to correct something right away, then you are complaining, and it only hurts your happiness. During the day, try to catch yourself each time you complain. Make a note of it. You can even journal it. The key is to be aware you are doing it.

2. Once you know how often you complain, the next step is to set a goal of how long you would like to go without complaining. Start small and set a goal of going 30 minutes without complaining. If you are successful, expand the goal to an hour, four hours, and so forth. However, don't be too quick to push the goal. I recommend going days at a time with one small goal. This will ensure you are truly meeting the goal, and it also gives you the opportunity to practice the Stop-It Technique.

3. Happiness with a Friend: Your "Happiness Friend" might be someone you have shared complaints with from time to time. After all, it's quite normal to open up to a friend and express frustrations. Your assignment, though, is to turn the tables. Rather than complaining to your friend, talk openly with your friend about your own experience in trying to stop complaining. Another idea is to ask your friend to have a "Positive Venting" session, where you focus on great things around you and good things about

other people. (As an aside, gossiping about others is just another form of complaining.)

4. Once you have been practicing "not complaining" for a few weeks, come back to this book and, in the space below, write down your reflections. For example, you might write that you complain more (or less) than you expected or you might reflect on the difficulty of not "venting." The key is to be honest with yourself about your own experience.

NOTES

STOP WORRYING

*"Worrying does not take away tomorrow's troubles.
It takes away today's peace."*
— RANDY ARMSTRONG[32]

Nothing drains your joy like worry. Ask any parents whose daughter recently got her license and heads out in the family car for the evening. With the house to themselves, the parents plan a quiet evening at home with a nice meal and a movie. However, as the evening progresses, the parents start to worry, and their worry becomes consuming. They wonder how she is doing, if she is speeding, and whether other drivers are watching out for her. They are too distracted to enjoy the evening they planned. The worry is just too great, and they can't release that worry until the moment the daughter turns into the driveway.

There are, of course, even more serious scenarios, such as waiting for the results of a biopsy, wondering if your relationship is in trouble, or having uncertainty about the security of your job. The worry in these scenarios can be so intense that it completely disrupts your day-to-day routine. You might be at the grocery store and forget what you wanted to buy simply because your mind is so consumed with worry.

Worrying can be one of the most debilitating and harmful

forces in life. It can drain your energy, cause you to lose focus, and, if excessive, block you from true happiness and even harm your health. Research shows worry can cause:[33]

- Fatigue
- Irritability
- Headaches
- Rapid Heartbeat
- Inability to Focus
- Coronary Disease
- Memory Loss

To be happier, you must steer your subconscious toward positivity and beauty, but worrying can block your ability to do that. Worry not only occupies your mind and blocks it from focusing on positivity; worry also redirects your focus. By its very nature, worry is a focus on something negative, and in your quest for happiness, you want to focus on positive things. If your mind is consumed with the thought, "What if the test results show my mother has cancer" or "How will I pay my bills if I lose my job," then it is virtually impossible to see all the beauty around you. Allowing your mind to be consumed with worry is the opposite of what is needed for long-term happiness.

You need to reduce or remove worry to be happier, but worry is a behavior learned over many years and is therefore difficult to control. Wouldn't it be nice if you could just tell yourself, "Stop worrying," and you did stop worrying? Unfortunately, it's not quite this simple and requires some more powerful tools

My father would offer such wisdom as, "Why worry about

a problem you don't have?" or "How will worry help your problem?" He also would say that most things people worry about never come true. This last gem of wisdom was proven by a study at Penn State University. In the study, participants were asked to write down their worries for a 30-day period. The results of the study showed that 91% of what participants worried about never came true. Even for those things that did come true, I doubt worrying helped any of them.[34]

Worry is harmful to your health, can block your happiness, and as revealed in the Penn State study, is usually related to something that never happens. Why, then, do people worry? Why would they do something that is both illogical and harmful? The reason people worry is they see it as a way to cope with their problems. They see worrying as addressing the issue by thinking about it. And when they do this repeatedly over time, worry becomes part of their subconscious, and the worry cycle begins.

Let's say you have a presentation in three weeks. If you are like most people, you hate public speaking, so you are immediately worried about it. You start thinking, "Oh, I hate speaking in front of people. I just dread giving that presentation." As the day of your presentation gets closer, you start thinking about the presentation itself, which is logical, because you need to start preparing. You need to consider what your specific topic will be, how much time you will speak, and the details of what you will say. These are necessary steps and can even reduce your worry. Unfortunately, though, you also start thinking:

- "What if I mess up in front of everybody?"
- "What if I lose my place?"

- "I hope I won't look nervous."
- "I hope they don't see my hands shaking."

Your mind has moved away from preparation mode to worry mode. As the day of your presentation draws even closer, you might start losing sleep or having trouble focusing. You are now in the worry cycle.

People try to explain their worry habits by saying, "I'm just a worrier" or "I can't help it." Neither of these statements is true. You don't have to be a worrier, and yes, you can help it. Much like happiness itself, worry is a choice. It is a habit that is learned over time, but once you realize you can do something about it, then you can either choose to continue worrying, and possibly causing great harm to yourself, or you can choose not to worry and enjoy life to its fullest.

Let's equip you with the tools to significantly reduce, or even eliminate, worry from your life. In the chapter on complaining, I introduced the "Stop-It Technique," a variation of the "Shut-Up Technique." The Shut-Up Technique serves as a powerful first step in managing worry. When you feel yourself starting to worry, the first step is awareness and shutting down your subconscious. Telling yourself to "shut up" reinforces to your subconscious you are aware of what is happening, and you are ready to take control. Speaking the words aloud adds power to the message.

Telling yourself to shut up starts to shut down your subconscious, but it is not sufficient to completely break the worry cycle. In the early stages of overcoming worry, you should tell yourself to shut up and then take additional control by telling yourself you will worry about your situation at a given time. For example, assume you are sitting in a coffee shop, and you start worrying about that presentation you are going to give in a few weeks. Your mind is consumed with thoughts of messing up, being embarrassed, getting tough questions, or being ill-prepared. At this point, you should stop anything else you are doing, tell yourself to shut up, and then tell yourself the exact time you will worry. By setting a time, you are telling your subconscious you are the one in charge of your life. You should also set a limit on how much time you will worry. For example, if I were in this scenario, I might say, "Ken, shut up! I'm going to worry about this for 15 minutes at 7 o'clock." I then would take out my phone and set a calendar reminder for 7:00 p.m. When 7:00 p.m. rolls around, I would set my timer for 15 minutes.

Employing this process is a way of weaning yourself off the worry cycle. You don't have to go "cold turkey," instead, you allow yourself to worry for a bit, and after you do, you can get back to living your life. The process takes time and patience to be effective. In the current scenario, you might finish worrying at 7:15 and then find yourself in the worry cycle again at 9:00 p.m. As you may have guessed, you would once again use the shut-up technique and set another time.

The next step in managing worry is to convert worry into action. When someone tells me they are worried, I will ask, "What are you going to do about it?" They typically respond in one of two ways. For example, if you told me you were worried about your annual review at work next week, and I asked what you are going to do about it, you might tell me, "There is nothing I can do." My mind then goes back to my father's advice when he asked the rhetorical question, "How will worry improve your situation?" In the case of your upcoming annual review, I realize your options are limited and there is little you can do at this point. I might ask what you would do in the worst-case scenario. What would you do if your annual review is horrible? Would you want to leave your job? What job options do you have? Would you want to improve and get better next year? Once you have considered what you would do in the worst-case scenario, you frankly have nothing left to consider. In other words, you have no other actions to take, so worrying will not improve your situation.

If you are worrying about your upcoming presentation, your response might be different when I ask what you are going to do about it. Maybe there is something you could do. You could review your topic some more, think through the details of the talk, or discuss your topic with someone else. (You might notice I didn't mention you could rehearse your talk, because I instruct people to use something other than "rehearsing" when it comes to public speaking. But that is a topic for another time, or another book.)

When you are able to take action, you can change the sequence for the shut-up technique. In the case of your upcoming presentation, you tell yourself to shut up and then say, "I'm going to work on my presentation at 6 o'clock tonight." A little worry can actually be helpful if you learn how to turn it into action. The key, though, is to stop with action and not allow yourself to drift into worry after you have decided on your actions.

Worry is one of the most debilitating forces in life. I have watched people, including people in my own family, become consumed with worry. It dramatically restricts your happiness and can be very harmful to your health. Learning to stop the cycle of worry is one of the greatest gifts you can give yourself. I can confess I personally had a habit of worrying but overcame that habit many years ago. I am amazed at how empowering it feels not to have worry controlling my life.

STOP WORRYING
ASSIGNMENTS

1. The very first thing to do in this lesson is learn how to tell yourself to Shut Up! As soon as you realize you are starting to worry, tell yourself to shut up. Don't think about the next step yet. Just practice listening to yourself and your inner voice and immediately and emphatically tell yourself to shut up.

2. Once you learn to tell yourself to shut up, the next step is to take control and set a time to either worry or take action. The key is to set a time. Just try it. Even if you don't do anything at that time, just practice telling yourself to shut up and setting a time. Once you have tried this a few times, you can start using the designated time to take action or continue to worry. Be sure to set a timer, though. Don't allow yourself to get back into an endless loop of worry. You are effectively telling your subconscious brain it is your turn to take over and to do things on your schedule. When the timer goes off, move on with your day. The sequence of telling yourself to shut

up, setting a time, using the time as you see fit, and then stopping the worry is quite powerful. Eventually, you will have trained your subconscious that continuing to worry without action is futile and even harmful, and you will instinctively stop worrying.

3. Happiness with a Friend: A friend can be a great sounding board for worry. Be open to hearing each other's worries. Sometimes just verbalizing your worries to another person can help. Also, be open to ask questions of each other, such as (1) what can you do about the situation (if there is something, that's great, but otherwise, worry doesn't help), (2) what is the worst that can happen, (3) can you handle the worst-case scenario, and (4) how can I help?

4. In the space below, write down how well you did with (1) learning to tell yourself to Shut Up, (2) scheduling time for worry, (3) moving on after the designated time. Regardless of how well you do, you must give yourself time and grace. Worrying is one of those habits you have perfected over a lifetime. Old habits take time to break.

NOTES

BUILD STRONG
RELATIONSHIPS

"Loneliness kills. It's as powerful as smoking or alcoholism."
— ROBERT WALDINGER[35]

You may have heard the expression, "Loneliness kills." Unfortunately, it's true. Researchers have studied the effect of loneliness on health, and the findings are frightening. For example, one study found:

> The long-term health consequences of loneliness and insufficient social connection include a 29% increased risk of heart disease, a 32% increased risk of stroke and a 50% increased risk of developing dementia in older adults, according to the surgeon general. People who frequently feel lonely are also more likely to develop depression and other mental health challenges, compared to people who rarely or never feel lonely.[36]

Other studies have shown loneliness results in a 14% higher risk of death, isolation results in a 32% higher risk of death, and individuals with a subjective feeling of loneliness had a 26% increase in the likelihood of death. This evidence shows loneliness and social isolation are harmful to your health and even increase your risk of dying. As you might expect, loneliness and social isolation are also associated with lower levels of happiness, well-being, and life satisfaction.[37]

On a more positive note, developing strong relationships may be the most important thing you do in your lifetime. Strong personal relationships are associated with long-term health and greater happiness. To be more specific, strong relationships are associated with:

- Longer life expectancy
- Higher self-esteem
- Improved mental health
- Reduced stress
- Improved coping mechanisms
- More resilience
- Better academic performance
- Better workplace performance[38]

The greatest proof of the power of strong relationships is from the longest research study in history, the Harvard study on what makes a good life. In 1938, a group of Harvard researchers embarked on one of the greatest studies of all time, and the study continues to this day. The researchers wanted to investigate what factors are associated with a good life.[39]

The original study began as two studies: one with a group of 19-year-old young men from Harvard (which was an all-male institution at the time) and the other study with a group of young juvenile delinquents from nearby South Boston. The purpose of the study was to investigate what makes people thrive. The researchers followed the participants through every phase of life, from young adulthood to end-of-life. As the participants aged, the researchers included the original participants' offspring and others, and the study now has grown from its original 795 participants to 1300. The research study continues to this day, with the two original studies now combined into one. The researchers have examined every aspect of the subjects' lives. They have conducted interviews, analyzed blood samples, and performed brain scans. They "tracked the same individuals, asking thousands of questions and taking hundreds of measurements."[40]

The Harvard study generated powerful and unequivocal findings. For example, if I were to ask you to tell me the factors that lead to a long, healthy life, I would expect you to emphasize genetics, diet, and exercise. Surprisingly, though, the Harvard study revealed the real key to a long and happy life is good strong relationships:

"In fact, good relationships are significant enough that if we had to take all eighty-four years of the Harvard Study and boil it down to a single principle for living, one life investment that is supported by similar findings across a wide variety of other studies, it would be this: Good relationships keep us healthier and happier. Period. So if you're going to make that one choice, that single decision that could best ensure your own health and happiness, science tells us that your choice should be to cultivate warm relationships."[41]

In the early part of this chapter, we emphasized the dangers of loneliness and just now revealed the importance of good relationships. The lesson is simple; building strong relationships leads to a longer and happier life. Therefore, you must put considerable time and effort into developing personal relationships and nurturing those relationships.

It is easy to find reasons not to take the trip with friends or to schedule a time to invite a friend out for a glass of wine or to call that old friend you haven't talked to in years. However, just like all the lessons in this book, you need to make a conscious decision to make a dedicated effort to live the life you want to live, and you must therefore make the effort to connect to friends. You will be glad you did. Every time you have a memorable moment with someone close to you, you are adding levels of happiness and years to your life.

Some of you might feel all hope is lost because you are getting older and your close relationships are dwindling or are gone altogether. Perhaps your closest relationship was with a spouse, and that person is no longer in your life, or you had good close friends where you used to live but they are now hundreds of miles away. The good news is that it's never too late to develop close relationships. Building new relationships can seem daunting, but you will be surprised how little effort is required. Rather than sitting at home, go out one night a week to a special-interest club, such as a group supporting animal welfare, art, food, or exercise. Put yourself in places where other people are. And when someone says, "we should all get together for dinner," Go! You might feel awkward at first, but it becomes easier and more natural. Remember you are giving yourself the wonderful gift of a long life and a happier life.

BUILD STRONG RELATIONSHIPS
ASSIGNMENTS

1. Just as you might create a Balance Sheet to assess your financial status, you should similarly create a "Relationship Balance Sheet" to assess your relationships. Write a list of your relationships, including friends and family. This is not a list of your Facebook or Instagram friends; this is a list of people you truly care for and who care for you. You should then categorize that Relationships Balance Sheet by the closeness of the relationships, with the closest at the top. Be grateful for any relationships you have; they all make your life better but pay special attention to those in the "very close" category. These are the people you can talk to about anything, be vulnerable to, and cry with. If you have even one or two people in this category, you are truly fortunate. Once you create your Relationship Balance Sheet, reflect on it and realize this is the true measure of wealth in your life.

2. Now it's time to take the initiative and develop or cultivate your relationships. It's quite easy to get caught up in day-to-day activities and not prioritize relationships; however, relationships need to be a priority as much as your job or family. You should always have short-term plans to do something for enjoyment with other people. This could be going to a concert or a dinner with friends in the next week or two. You should also have at least one long-term plan to do something special with other people. This could include planning a trip with others or a

big party. By making plans, you are making relationships a priority. Also, you will find anticipating an event is a wonderful part of the enjoyment. As my mother (Ashley's "Grandmother Kitty") would say, "Anticipation is greater than participation," and as usual, she was right.

3. Happiness with a Friend: Any assignment here would simply be redundant.

4. In the space below, be accountable to yourself. Write down things you plan to do with friends in the next 6 months. These can be small events, like going out for dinner, or big events, like taking a cruise. Just be sure to set short-term and long-term goals!

NOTES

SAY THANK YOU

"The more we say thanks, the more we find to be thankful for."
— DOUGLAS WOOD [42]

I have delivered hundreds of happiness speeches for more than 15 years, and I have given countless bits of advice on how to be happier. The one piece of advice I have given more than any other is the simple lesson of saying "Thank You." It sounds so simple, but the advice is sincere, and the effect is strong.

The ultimate goal of this book is to teach you how to retrain your subconscious to be happier. Do you remember Sarah and the Cold Green Beans Effect? Sarah was your friend from lunch who just seemed naturally focused on anything negative and even focused on something so insignificant as the temperature of her green beans. After many years of training, Sarah's subconscious was focused on the negative, and chances are she didn't even realize it.

Like Sarah, you have many thoughts going through your subconscious that you also are not aware of. You might feel unhappy, but chances are you blame your life circumstances without realizing your subconscious is to blame. The lessons in this book will help you take control of your subconscious, retrain it, and be happier. I think this lesson about saying thank you is probably the most powerful.

My friend Shelly (not her real name) sent me an email a few years ago saying, "Ken, I know you go all over the world and talk about happiness. I'm not happy. What is the secret." I quickly wrote back and said, "Shelly, the ultimate secret to happiness is learning to say thank you." Shelly sent an equally quick reply saying, "Ken, I'm a polite southern woman. I always say please and thank you." My email back to her was swift and was the last in the chain. It simply said, "Shelly, you have to mean it."

When I tell you to say thank you, I am telling you to be specific and deliberate. And be authentic. In other words, you don't just occasionally say an empty thank you. You should instead use the following thank-you guidelines:

- Say it often, very often. In fact, say it so often that it's weird.
- Be specific about what you are thanking the person for.
- Be authentic. People don't want flattery; they want sincerity.

What is the first thing you do when you start work in the morning? If you are like most people, you sit at your desk, open your email, gasp when you see the list of new emails, and think, "Oh no, I have a lot of work to do." You then start plugging away at those email messages, just trying to reduce the number in your Inbox.

I suggest you try this instead. When you arrive at your office or sit down at your desk in the morning, make it a point to tell someone thank you. Rather than hammering out responses to emails, open a blank email and send someone a note of thanks. Remember to be specific and be authentic. You might write a message that says, "Robin, that was a very tense meeting yesterday with a lot of emotions in the room. I was very impressed by the way you took control and brought everyone together. You showed great leadership. Thank you." Or, better yet, walk down the hall, walk in Robin's door, and say it in person.

Later in the day, when you are going through the check-out lane at the grocery store, push yourself to find something to be thankful for. I recently went through the check-out line at my local Costco. They had one employee ringing up my (too many) items and another employee quickly placing my items in the basket. They were amazingly efficient. I told each of them how amazed I was at their efficiency and how much I appreciated them. I was sincere; it was an amazing feat to behold. Admittedly, it was just a small expression of appreciation, but I hope it made them feel good. I knew it made me feel good to say it and was one more step in training my subconscious to focus on the positive. It was one more step in my quest to be happier.

The list above tells you to say it so often that you "make it weird." I want you to make every attempt to say thank you as often as you can, and I want you to become obsessed with it. Make it your mission to express gratitude toward others throughout the day. Yes, it will feel weird, but the rewards are wonderful.

When you are deliberately, and weirdly often, finding things to say thank you about, you are retraining your subconscious to focus on things to be thankful for. After retraining, you will be driving down the road and subconsciously, instinctively, notice things to be thankful for: the sunset, the song you're listening to or the peace and quiet, the smile on your child's face in the back seat, or the excitement about the trip you are taking next month.

Do negative things exist? Of course they do, and you should do something about them when you can. But wouldn't you rather go through life focusing on the positive and being genuinely happy? I am sure you have seen those people who always seem happy, and you have thought to yourself, "I wish I had what they have." Guess what? Now you have what they have. You have the secrets to being genuinely happy.

Speaking of saying thank you, I would like to say "thank you" for reading this book. To think you took the time to read some of my thoughts is genuinely humbling, and I am more than grateful.

SAY THANK YOU
ASSIGNMENTS

1. Remember this will feel weird at first, but you must get started and stick with it. Set a goal of saying one extra "thank you" per day. It might be a special thank you to someone at work or a special thank you to a family member. Be deliberate and be authentic. The more you do it, the more it will become a habit.

2. Happiness with a Friend: This is a follow-up from one of the Stop Complaining assignments. Make time to meet with your friend and rather than venting or complaining,

focus on things you are thankful for. Expressing gratitude is more effective than just thinking about it. When meeting with your friend, be sure to elaborate on the expressions of gratitude and ask each other questions. Nothing is off limits when it comes to gratitude.

3. Saying thank you can be remarkably effective for increasing your happiness. Writing down expressions of gratitude can also be highly effective. After you have been deliberate in saying thank you for a few weeks, come back here and use the space below to record expressions of gratitude. They can be small things, such as someone holding a door open for you today, or big things like meeting your new grandchild for the first time. Everything counts. Remember the key is to retrain your subconscious so you automatically focus on things to be thankful for. You will also notice we have given you extra pages here, because we know there is always a lot to be thankful for.

NOTES

NOTES

NOTES

NOTES

WHAT MAKES YOU HAPPY? YOU!

You might have developed a habit of waking up every morning and working against your own happiness. The good news is you now can change that cycle, and you are the only one who can. Much like my daughters retraining their subconscious minds to play beautiful music on the piano, you can retrain your subconscious to have a beautiful, happy life. You now understand what does, and does not, make you happy and you have five lessons to practice each day. Please practice the five lessons. With effort and consistency, you will be happier very soon, and with additional practice, your happiness will continue to grow. Please start the journey; it's a beautiful journey.

We wish you a long, happy life.

And...thank you!

ENDNOTES

1   Gilbert, Daniel. *Stumbling on Happiness.* New York: Knopf, 2006

2   Ibid, p. 23.

3   Barry, Dave. "Long ago, no one counted carbs." *The Laconia Daily Sun*, 28 Mar. 2004, laconiadailysun.com/opinion/colums/davebarry/article_92830989a9a8525e-87b4ad15148def31.html.

4   Stutzer, A., & Frey, B. S. (2008). *Stress that doesn't pay: The commuting paradox.* The Scandinavian Journal of Economics, 110(2), 339–366. https://doi.org/10.1111/j.1467-9442.2008.00542.x

5   Lyubomirsky, S. (2013). *The myths of happiness: What should make you happy, but doesn't; what shouldn't make you happy, but does.* Penguin Press.

6   Gilbert, Daniel. *Stumbling on Happiness.* New York: Knopf, 2006.

7   Ibid, p. 197.

8   Brickman, P., Coates, D., & Janoff-Bulman, R. (1978). *Lottery winners and accident victims: Is happiness relative?* Journal of Personality and Social Psychology, 36(8), 917–927. https://doi.org/10.1037/0022-3514.36.8.917

9   Ben-Shahar, T. (2007). *Happier: Learn the secrets to daily joy and lasting fulfillment.* McGraw-Hill.

10 Ibid.

11 Maslow, A. H. (1943). *A theory of human motivation. Psychological Review, 50*(4), 370–396. https://doi. org/10.1037/h0054346

12 Lyubomirsky, S., Sheldon, K. M., & Schkade, D. (2005). Pursuing happiness: The architecture of sustainable change. *Review of General Psychology, 9*(2), 111–131. https://doi.org/10.1037/1089-2680.9.2.111

13 Lyubomirsky, S., Sheldon, K. M., & Schkade, D. (2005). Pursuing happiness: The architecture of sustainable change. *Review of General Psychology, 9*(2), 111–131.

14 See examples of ranking methodologies at:

Helliwell, J. F., Layard, R., Sachs, J. D., De Neve, J.-E., Aknin, L. B., & Wang, S. (Eds.). (2025). *World happiness report 2025.* Wellbeing Research Centre, University of Oxford.

WalletHub. (2025, March 11). *Happiest cities in America.* WalletHub. Retrieved from https://wallethub.com/edu/happiest-places-to-live/32619

15 Helliwell, J. F., Layard, R., Sachs, J. D., De Neve, J.E., Aknin, L. B., & Wang, S. (Eds.). (2025). *World Happiness Report 2025.* Wellbeing Research Centre, University of Oxford

16 https://www.rd.com/article/happiest-state/#:~:text=How%20does%20the%20rest%20of%20America%20stack%20up?&text=After%20evaluating%20states%20across%2030,Louisiana:%2032.97

17 https://www.goodreads.com/author/quotes/10735787. Ralph_Marston#:~:text=Happiness%20is%20a%20 choice%20%E2%80%93%20not,Ralph%20Marston

18 Lipton, B. H. (2005). *The biology of belief: Unleashing the power of consciousness, matter & miracles.* Mountain of Love/Elite Books.

19 Bradberry, Travis, *How Complaining Rewires Your Brain for Negativity.* 2022. https://www.talentsmarteq.com/ how-complaining-rewires-your-brain-for-negativity/

20 Amen, D. G. (2023). *30% Happier in 30 Days: A Quick Start to a Happier, Healthier You.* Tyndale Refresh.

21 Note: This quote is widely attributed to Confucius, though no definitive primary source has been found to confirm authorship.

22 Bodhi, Bhikkhu, trans. *The Connected Discourses of the Buddha: A New Translation of the Samyutta Nikaya.* Wisdom Publications, 2000.

23 Angelou, Maya. *Wouldn't Take Nothing for My Journey Now.* Random House, 1993.

24 Carnegie, D. (1936). *How to win friends and influence people.* Simon & Schuster.

25 Alicke, M. D., Braun, J. C., Siegel, R., & others. (1992). Complaining behavior in social interaction. *Personality and Social Psychology Bulletin, 18*(3), 286–295. https://doi. org/10.1177/0146167292183004

26 Bowen, W. (2007). *A complaint free world: How to stop complaining and start enjoying the life you always wanted.* Doubleday.

27 Bowen, Will. *A Complaint Free World, Revised and Updated: Stop Complaining, Start Living (p. 13). Harmony/ Rodale. Kindle Edition.*

28 Ibid, p. 31.

29 Bradberry, Travis (2002).

30 Ibid.

31 Bowen, Will, (2007).

32 Armstrong, R. (n.d.). *Worrying does not take away tomorrow's troubles. It takes away today's peace.* [Quote]. Retrieved from the Goodreads quote collection

33 Bruce, Debra Fulghum, PhD, *How Worrying Affects the Body*, WebMD, November 22, 2024.

34 LaFrenier, Lucas S. and Michelle G. Newman, Exposing Worry's Deceit: Percentage of Untrue Worries in Generalized Anxiety Disorder Treatment, *Behavior Therapy*, Vol 51, May 2020, pp. 413-423.

35 Waldinger, R. (2015, November). *What makes a good life? Lessons from the longest study on happiness* [Video]. TED Conferences.

36 Penn State. "Short-term loneliness associated with physical health problems." ScienceDaily. ScienceDaily, 13 June 2024. <www.sciencedaily.com/releases/2024/06/240613140903.htm>

37 See the following studies:

Harris, Emily. "MetaAnalysis: Social Isolation, Loneliness Tied to Higher Mortality." *JAMA*, vol. 330, no. 3, July 18, 2023, p. 211. doi: 10.1001/jama.2023.11958.

HoltLunstad J, Smith TB, Baker M, Harris T, Stephenson D. Loneliness and Social Isolation as Risk Factors for Mortality: A MetaAnalytic Review. *Perspectives on Psychological Science.* 2015;10(2):227–237.

Olawa, B. D., Idemudia, E. S., Omolayo, B. O., & Azikiwe, J. C. (2023). Loneliness and happiness in the face of the COVID19 lockdown: Examining the pathways through somatic symptoms and psychological distress. *Health Psychology Open.* Advance online publication. https://doi.org/10.1177/20551029231206764

38 See the following studies:

Harris, M. A., & Orth, U. (2020). The link between self-esteem and social relationships: A meta-analysis of longitudinal studies. *Journal of Personality and Social Psychology, 119*(6), 1459–1477. https://doi.org/10.1037/pspp0000265

Luo, Y., Wang, H., Hu, M., & Zhang, D. (2022). Social support and mental health among left-behind children in rural China: A meta-analysis. *Frontiers in Psychiatry, 13,* 874905. https://doi.org/10.3389/fpsyt.2022.874905

Patalay, P., & Fitzsimons, E. (2021). Mental ill-health and well-being at age 17: Findings from the Millennium Cohort Study. *British Journal of Psychiatry Open, 7*(3), e67. https://doi.org/10.1192/bjo.2021.19

Holt-Lunstad, J., Smith, T. B., & Layton, J. B. (2010). Social relationships and mortality risk: A meta-analytic review. *PLoS Medicine, 7*(7), e1000316. https://doi.org/10.1371/journal.pmed.1000316

Brown, E. G., Gallagher, S., & Creaven, A. M. (2023). The role of close relationships in older adults' coping and subjective well-being during the COVID-19 pandemic. *Journal of Social and Personal Relationships, 40*(2), 506–528. https://doi.org/10.1177/02654075221146065

39 Waldinger, R. J., & Schulz, M. S. (2023). *The good life: Lessons from the world's longest scientific study of happiness.* Simon & Schuster.

40 Ibid, p. 10.

41 Ibid.

42 Wood, D. (2005). *The secret of saying thanks.* Simon & Schuster Books for Young Readers.

www.ingramcontent.com/pod-product-compliance
Lightning Source LLC
Chambersburg PA
CBHW071226090426
42736CB00014B/2984